INTERNATIONAL INEQUALITY
AND NATIONAL POVERTY

INTERNATIONAL INEQUALITY AND NATIONAL POVERTY

Keith Griffin

HOLMES & MEIER PUBLISHERS, INC.
New York

First published in the United States of America 1978 by
HOLMES & MEIER PUBLISHERS, INC.
30 Irving Place, New York, N.Y. 10003

Library of Congress Cataloging in Publication Data

Griffin, Keith B
  International inequality and national poverty.

  Bibliography: p.
  Includes index.
  1. Underdeveloped areas. 2. Poverty. 3. Income distribution. 4. International economic relations. I. Title.
HC59.7.G748 1978   330.9′172′4   78–7002
ISBN 0–8419–0394–8

Printed in Great Britain

TO JOHN

A deepened consciousness of their situation leads men to apprehend that situation as an historical reality susceptible of transformation.

Paulo Freire in
Pedagogy of the Oppressed

Contents

Acknowledgements

Thomas Balogh and Paul Streeten were the first to stimulate my interest in problems of international inequality. The whole of Part One can therefore be said to have been influenced by them, although they do not agree with all of the opinions expressed. The essay on the international transmission of inequality benefited from the comments and criticism of W. M. Corden, Dudley Seers, Paul Streeten, Frances Stewart and Rosemary Thorp. The essay on the multinational corporations was improved as a result of suggestions from Sanjaya Lall, E. L. H. Lee, Charles van Onselen, Samir Radwan and Raul Trajtenberg. I also wish to thank Thomas Balogh, Jeffrey James, R. W. Johnson and Frances Stewart for their comments on the chapter devoted to the new international economic order.

Part Two was much influenced by Azizur Rahman Khan. We worked closely together for eighteen months in Geneva on problems of rural poverty in Asia, and during that time several of my ideas became more clearly formulated as a result of his gentle but incisive probing. Aziz Khan is co-author of Chapter 6 and his responsibility for Chapter 7 is almost equally great. I am indebted to Thomas Balogh and Ajit Ghose for comments on the Appendix to Chapter 6, a paper originally presented at the Fifth World Congress of the International Economic Association in Tokyo in September 1977. John Enos, Ajit Ghose and Frances Stewart made useful comments on the essay on world hunger and Neville Maxwell was equally helpful in commenting on the paper on China.

I am grateful to the editors and publishers of *World Development*, the *Bulletin of the Oxford University Institute of Economics and Statistics* and *Development and Change* for permission to reprint material used previously.

Queen Elizabeth House, Oxford   *K. B. Griffin*
November 1977

Introduction

International Inequality and National Poverty is a collection of essays united by a common objective, namely, increasing our understanding of the multitude of forces which account for the persistence of poverty and growing inequality. The volume is divided into two parts. Part One contains a selection of papers concerned with international aspects of the problem; while Part Two contains papers in which national issues are discussed. Although national and international issues are treated separately, I hope to make clear below that there are in fact strong connections between them.

The intellectual origin of most writings on economic relations between rich and poor countries, at least in the West, is the Ricardian theory of comparative advantage and the refinements which have been made to it in the last 160 years. Writers whose work falls within this tradition usually argue that international economic interchange improves the world allocation of resources, raises average incomes in all participating countries and results in a faster rate of growth. Trade, capital movements and migrations of labour obey the principle of all-round advantage. There is another tradition, however, encompassing dissenters and radicals loosely bound together in being critical of the Ricardian theory and in emphasising the negative consequences that can arise from unrestricted intercourse for specific countries and groups of people. Writers in this tradition are linked together not by adherence to a single alternative theory but by an interest in a set of issues readily evoked by terms such as imperialism, neo-colonialism, dependence, unequal partners and unequal exchange.

The reader will find echoes of some of these phrases in the following chapters. The essence of the claim that is being made, however, is this: the presumption that unrestricted international intercourse will reduce inequality and poverty is not universally valid. It can be shown in theory and in history that such intercourse may accentuate inequality and even increase poverty. Indeed, it has become evident from the experience of the last few decades: first, that the absolute difference in income between the rich countries and the poor has increased dramatically; second, that

1

on balance the rate of growth of income per head has been positively associated with the level of income, so that relative inequality also has tended to increase;[1] and third, that the level of income of some of the poorest people in the poorest countries has declined absolutely.[2]

International integration has led to national disintegration and dependence in the Third World. This is reflected in growing national and international inequality, the absolute impoverishment of a minority in poor countries, and greater social differentiation among the ex-colonial people. At the same time the post-colonial international system has helped to create a harmony of interests between the élites of the Third World and those of the industrialized world,[3] and in the process a conflict of interests between rich countries and poor has been partially transformed into a conflict between the masses and the élite within the poor countries. On occasion this conflict has erupted into violent civil strife.[4]

One of the great differences between orthodox economists and the dissenters is that the analyses of the former tend to be couched either in terms of an individual (micro-economics) or in terms of a country as a whole (macro-economics). The dissenters, in contrast, usually assume that class divisions are important, that different classes have different interests and that the effects of economic phenomena on the distribution of income are at least as important as their effects on the level of income and its rate of growth. The neo-classical orthodoxy, in other words, implicitly assumes a classless society,[5] whereas the dissenters take their inspiration from the classical economists and explicitly assume that society does not consist of a homogeneous collection of individuals but of separate and identifiable classes.[6] This volume contains several essays in which class distinctions are central to the analysis, e.g. in determining the causes of hunger or the effects of large scale migrations of labour.[7]

A second great difference follows almost automatically from the use of class analysis. The dissenters assume that political and economic power are always present to some degree and consequently that monopoly and monopsony elements, and similar phenomena, must be taken into account when examining the effects, say, of an integrated international economy on world development. Orthodox economists, on the other hand, frequently assume that power is absent and that something approximating perfect competition prevails.[8] When it comes to the multinational enterprises, for example, economists like myself argue that often the bargaining strength of the corporations is substantially greater than that of the local government.[9] Orthodox economists such as a distinguished former professor at Oxford reply that 'there was never a tittle of truth' in this generalisation. [10] Such discrepant views arise not from the fact that Professor Little and I may rely on different sources of information, but from the fact that we rely on a different theory or paradigm to interpret information.

A third major difference has to do with the treatment of time. Orthodox analysis is essentially timeless; little interest is shown in history. Much effort is devoted to an exploration of the characteristics of static equilibria and, even when the time dimension is introduced, it is done so in a highly formal way merely by adding subscripts of t or $(t + 1)$ to variables in an equation. Technical change is often treated as occurring randomly and without bias, as being easily spread and hence as unambiguously beneficial.

The dissenters are less interested in mathematical time than in historical time. Rather than focus on states of equilibrium, they are more likely to assume that the international economy is in dynamic disequilibrium, continuously striving without success to adjust to shocks and disturbances and achieve a position of stable equilibrium. The spirit of this approach is exemplified in Chapter 1. It is there postulated that technical change is the engine of the world economy, and it is argued that new technology is created systematically, that most of this occurs in the industrial countries, that this introduces a strong disequilibrating element into the world economy and sets in motion forces which tend to increase international inequality. [11]

Some of these points are now becoming recognised. For example, in a recent book on *Rich and Poor Countries* it is claimed that the 'fundamental advantage of the rich countries is . . . that they are the home of modern technology . . . . The real source of the maldistribution of the gains from trade and investment lies in the nature of modern technology and the process of its development.' The authors conclude that 'salvation lies . . . in the development of indigenous scientific and technological capacities within the developing countries and in a reorientation of the present system of research and development which by and large ignores their needs.' [12]

The effect of technical change in rich countries is to raise the profit rate in rich countries (and of their multinational corporations operating in poor countries) above the rate obtainable by local entrepreneurs in poor countries. There is of course no direct causal relationship between expenditure on research and development (R & D) and the rate of profit, but 'regression analysis of cross-sections of individual industry groups and of firms enabled investigators to obtain confirmation of the hypothesis that productivity-increases, as estimated by the method of the Residual, are positively correlated with R & D – intensity.'[13]

Neo-classical theory would lead one to predict that because of the scarcity of capital in underdeveloped countries the rate of return on capital would be higher in poor countries than in rich. Our theory, in contrast, would lead one to predict that because of the concentration of new technology in the rich countries the marginal returns to capital (as well as to labour) would be relatively low in the poor countries. There is not sufficient evidence to resolve this dispute, but it is perhaps instructive to note that several orthodox economists have also come to the conclusion that the return on investment is higher in developed than in underdeveloped economies. Thus Stolper notes that it is 'extra-ordinarily difficult to find a great number of projects that could pay even 6 per cent, let alone the 10 per cent or 15 per cent often suggested.'[14] Johnson claims it is a 'reasonable assumption' that the return on investment is normally greater in the developed countries,[15] and Schmitt concludes from his survey of the literature that 'there is in fact a presumption that rates of return must be lower in backward than in progressive economies.'[16]

If one combines these two pieces of information, namely, that technical change is concentrated in the rich countries and that this raises the profit rate or return on investment there, it can readily be shown that, in a world in which finance capital or savings are free to move, the poor countries will be harmed. The easiest way to show this is with a diagram first developed by Walter Eltis to explore the relationship between profits and growth in a single economy.[17]

In Figure 1 $r_m K$ is the investment function. It indicates the rate of accumulation of capital that will be forthcoming for a given rate of profit; r_m is the minimum rate of profit necessary before any investment takes place. For the sake of simplicity it is assumed the investment function is the same initially in both developed d and underdeveloped countries u.

NN is an investment opportunity function, also assumed to be initially the same in both countries. The investment opportunity function indicates the 'trade-off' or inverse relationship between the rate of growth of the stock of capital g and the rate of profit r. That is, the function illustrates the idea that for any given level of technology and size of the labour force, the faster capital is accumulated, the lower the rate of return on investment will be. If the labour force were to grow or labour-augmenting technical change were to occur, the entire function would shift to the right.

The intersection of the two functions determines the rate of profit r_1

and rate of growth of the capital stock g_1 that will prevail initially in both countries. Given our assumptions, both the developed and underdeveloped country would grow at the same pace and experience the same rate of return.

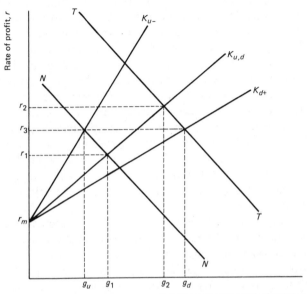

FIGURE 1

Suppose, now, that labour-augmenting technical change occurs in the developed country only. This has the effect of shifting the investment opportunity function of the developed country to, say, TT, thereby raising the rate of profit in that country to r_2. The higher profit rate, in turn, leads to a higher level of national savings, an acceleration in the pace of capital formation to g_2 and a correspondingly faster rate of growth of output. Income per head begins to grow faster in the developed than in the underdeveloped country and international income inequality increases.

If the process were to stop here the poor countries would have few grounds for complaint since the rich countries could claim, correctly, that the acceleration of their growth rate was not at the expense of growth in the poor countries but originated entirely from their own efforts to generate new technology. Unfortunately, however, the process does not stop here, for the configuration of r_2 and g_2 is a disequilibrium situation.

Technical change in the rich country raises the rate of profit in that country above the rate prevailing in the poor country. If both economies were closed this would not matter, but in the context of an integrated world capitalist economy the differential profit rate $r_2 - r_1$ would constitute a strong and clear signal to savers in the poor country to transfer their finance capital to the rich. Investment resources would tend to shift from low- to high-income countries in an attempt to eliminate the disequilibrium. The attempt might never succeed, as new bursts of technical change might continuously interfere with a smooth adjustment, but in the process of seeking a new equilibrium the rate of growth would be further accelerated in the rich countries and reduced in the poor. This would add another twist to international inequality and undermine the claims made in the previous paragraph: growth in the rich countries would be partly at the expense of growth in the poor.

Assuming a new equilibrium is achieved, in terms of our diagram the world economy would eventually settle down to a uniform rate of profit of r_3 and a growth rate of the capital stock of g_d in the rich country and g_u in the poor, where $g_d > g_u$.

The consequences of the slower rate of growth in the underdeveloped country would not be felt equally by all members of society. During the transition from a growth rate of g_1 to g_u the rate of profit would be rising and, assuming a constant capital–output ratio, the share of profits in total income would be rising as well. This implies that income from profits in the underdeveloped country would grow more rapidly than total income. Conversely, during the transition the share of wages in total income would be falling and the growth of wage income would be slower than the average and, of course, considerably slower than the growth of income from profits. In other words, the entire burden of adjustment in the poor country would fall on the working class.[18] At the end of the transition their share of income and the rate of growth of their income would be lower than before. The capitalist class, on the other hand, would enjoy a higher share of the total income of the poor country, a higher return on their investments and a faster rate of growth of the income from their combined assets in rich and poor countries. It is no wonder that the élites of underdeveloped countries are often allied with those of the developed ones!

Foreign aid can be viewed as an attempt to offset, in whole or in part, the disequalising tendencies of the international economy and in particular to compensate the poor of the Third World for the loss of part of the investible surplus to the developed countries. Such reasoning could provide a moral case for the rich countries to give resources to the poor, but it is unlikely that it has ever provided a practical case for doing so. Indeed, the contribution of foreign aid to the alleviation of poverty in the Third World has at best been slight and at worst negative. It may be harsh to claim that foreign aid is part of the disequalising system rather than an offset to it, but there are numerous indicators which point in that direction.

First, the amount of aid is very small, viz. at present little more than a third of one per cent of the gross national product of the donor countries.[19] Never, in fact, has so much been written about so little. Second, much of the aid disbursed since the end of the Second World War has gone to the less-poor countries. For example, during the period 1945 to 1970 Europe was by far the largest recipient of US aid, with 35.2 per cent of the total, receiving exactly the same amount as South Asia, the Near East and Latin America combined. Britain alone received 60 per cent more than the whole of Africa! Viewing the Third World in isolation, it is well known that foreign aid has been channelled disproportionately to the relatively prosperous countries. Large and very poor countries such as India and Bangladesh have received far less aid than either their numbers or their need would suggest as equitable. Third, there is no evidence that within the poor countries the aid has, on balance, gone to the poorest people. On the contrary, the recent attempts by various international agencies to devise new lending and development policies—the IBRD's emphasis on the poorest 40 per cent of the population, the ILO's call for a 'basic needs' strategy of development, UNICEF's stress on 'basic services', etc.—suggest that the donors, too, have begun to recognise that aid has failed to reach those most in need.

Fourth, a significant proportion of such aid as has been transferred to the Third World has been used to supplement consumption rather than investment and consequently the impact of aid on the rate of growth has usually been rather small.[20] Another way of saying the same thing is that foreign aid has tended to depress the savings ratio in the recipient countries. In effect, underdeveloped countries have borrowed capital in part to increase their consumption.

This would not matter very much if two provisos were met, namely, (i) that the terms on which aid is supplied are sufficiently generous so that loans can easily be repaid and (ii) the savings ratio quickly recovers if and when aid ceases. In the absence of these provisos, aid is more likely to become the opium of the governments of poor countries than a stimulant to the economy or a purge of poverty.

There is, alas, evidence that neither proviso holds. An increasing number of Third World countries have encountered problems in financing their debts and several, particularly those which have experienced rapid rates of domestic inflation, have either defaulted or had to renegotiate their external loans. If most of the foreign aid had been invested and if the investments had yielded a rate of return in excess of the interest rate on foreign borrowing, there should have been no debt-servicing problems. The fact that there have been such problems is strong prima facie evidence that foreign capital has often not been used productively.[21] It has supplemented unproductive consumption and in the process reduced the rate of savings.

The question then arises as to what happens to savings when aid-inflows stop. Grinols and Bhagwati tried to shed some light on this by constructing a formal model and simulating the behaviour of the economy of 17 underdeveloped countries. They assumed capital inflows were equivalent to 5 per cent of national product and asked of their model how many years would be required for a country's savings in the presence of a capital inflow to recover to the *level* that would have prevailed in the absence of foreign capital. The answer varied considerably from one country to another, but the unweighted mean for the 17 countries analysed was 'just over 40 years!'[22] That is, after the cessation of foreign aid and other forms of capital inflow, it takes about four decades on average, or an entire generation, for the level of savings in a country to recover to what it would have been had there never been any aid.

More significant is what happens to the *ratio* of savings to national product, since it is this ratio which largely determines a country's rate of growth. Here Grinols and Bhagwati find that in only two cases did the savings ratio ever recover.[23] That is, in the majority of countries studied dependence on foreign aid permanently lowered the country's capacity for self-reliant growth.

Ultimately, it seems clear, it is events in the domestic economy that determine whether the standard of living of poor people in poor countries rises or falls. There is some evidence that living standards of some of the most impoverished groups have actually fallen, although this view is disputed by many. It is not terribly important, however, whether the level of income of the poor has risen fractionally, remained unchanged or declined, the undeniable fact is that large numbers of people have experienced no discernible improvement in their real income for years on end.

It is tempting when confronted with the appallingly low levels of consumption of many groups in the Third World to take an absolutist view of poverty, i.e. to define the poor as those whose income or consumption falls below a particular level. In my opinion, however, this would be a mistaken approach. Even in the poorest countries, poverty is inescapably a relative concept and is therefore inextricably bound up with the distribution of income.[24] One could and should go further, however, and relate poverty to the structure of the society, a consequence of differences in the terms on which various groups or classes have access to sources of economic and political power.[25]

The poorest people in most underdeveloped countries are almost totally lacking in both economic and political power. They possess few skills and less wealth. There is little demand for their labour and the possibility of uniting in trade associations or labour unions to create effective bargaining power is slight. Politically, 'they are too heterogeneous in everything except their poverty, and for the most part too isolated and submerged at the bottom of the rural power structures, to be able to unite other than locally and ephemerally to improve their lot. The main forms of protest accessible to them are demonstrations, riots, land seizures and votes for populist candidates, and these expedients are most of the time in most local settings too ineffective or too dangerous to be resorted to.'[26] In other words, the poor are poor because of the way they are integrated into their society and economy. They will not cease to be poor until the economy and the polity are reorganised and the rules by which the fruits of the earth are distributed are altered.

NOTES AND REFERENCES

1. See Ch. 5.
2. See Chs. 6 and 7.
3. This point has been emphasised by Johan Galtung in his 'A Structural Theory of Imperialism', *Journal of Peace Research*, No. 2 (1971).
4. See, for example, E. Wayne Nafziger and William L. Richter, 'Biafra and Bangladesh: The Political Economy of Secessionist Conflict', *Journal of Peace Research*, No. 2 (1976).
5. An important exception is the neo-classical analysis of the effects of tariffs on the distribution of income. See W. F. Stolper and P. A. Samuelson, 'Protection and Real Wages', *Review of Economic Studies* (1941).
6. The roots of neo-classical trade theory are to be found in Chapter VII ('On Foreign Trade') of David Ricardo's *Principles of Political Economy and Taxation* (1817), whereas the class analysis of the dissenters has its origin in the first sentence of the 'Preface' to that book: 'The produce of the earth—all that is derived from its surface by the united application of labour, machinery, and capital—is divided among three classes of the community,

namely, the proprietor of the land, the owner of the stock or capital necessary for its cultivation, and the labourers by whose industry it is cultivated.'

7. See Chs. 8 and 4, respectively.

8. An exception is the neo-classical analysis of the effects of tariffs on a country's terms of trade. See Nicholas Kaldor, 'A Note on Tariffs and the Terms of Trade', *Economica* (Nov. 1940).

9. See Ch. 2.

10. I. M. D. Little, 'Gasping at Griffin', mimeographed notes, Hilary Term 1974, Nuffield College, Oxford, p. 3.

11. This view was whimsically presented by D. H. Robertson, who was neither a dissenter nor a radical, in his famous parable of the scientist and his servant. See Sir Dennis Robertson, *Britain in the World Economy*, (London: Allen and Unwin, 1954) pp. 58–9.

12. Hans Singer and Javed Ansari, *Rich and Poor Countries* (London: Allen and Unwin, 1977) p. 37.

13. William Fellner, 'Trends in the Activities Generating Technological Progress', *American Economic Review* (Mar. 1970) p. 10.

14. Wolfgang Stolper, *Planning Without Facts: Lessons in Resource Allocation from Nigeria's Development* (Harvard University Press, 1966) p. 198.

15. Harry G. Johnson, *Economic Policies Toward Less Developed Countries* (Washington: Brookings Institution, 1967) p. 123. See also, by the same author, *Technology and Economic Interdependence* (London: Macmillan for the Trade Policy Research Centre, 1975).

16. Hans O. Schmitt, 'Development Assistance: The View from Bretton Woods', *Public Policy* (Fall 1973) p. 593.

17. Walter Eltis, *Growth and Distribution* (London: Macmillan, 1973) p. 213.

18. This could be mitigated if members of the working class of poor countries were allowed to migrate *en masse* to the rich ones. See Ch. 4.

19. See Ch. 5.

20. See Ch. 3.

21. See the Appendix to Ch. 3.

22. E. Grinols and J. Bhagwati, 'Foreign Capital, Savings and Dependence', *Review of Economics and Statistics* (Nov. 1976) p. 421.

23. Ibid., p. 422.

24. This argument is presented at length in Ch. 7.

25. See the final paragraphs of Ch. 6.

26. Marshall Wolfe, 'Poverty as a Social Phenomenon and as a Central Issue for Development Policy', Social Development Division, U.N. Economic Commission for Latin America, ECLA/Draft/DS/133, mimeo (Apr. 1976) p. 14.

Part One

International Inequality

1. The international transmission of inequality

The point of departure of our analysis is the assumption that the motor of change in the contemporary world economy is technical innovation. There is growing evidence that the discovery and introduction of new techniques of production and of new products are major determinants of the pace and direction of economic expansion. The pattern and speed of expansion, in turn, affect the international distribution of income, the extent and location of poverty, and the general well-being of most of the world's inhabitants.

The primacy of technology has not always been acknowledged. Many economic historians, of course, particularly those writing about the industrial revolution in Europe, have attributed considerable importance to improvements in techniques and products. Among the theorists, Joseph Schumpeter was notable for his emphasis on discontinuous technological changes: 'Add successively as many mail coaches as you please, you will never get a railway thereby.'[1] The majority of economists, however, have made few systematic attempts to incorporate technological change into their theories explaining the behaviour of the economy, at least until quite recently.

The main body of formal literature on the theory of international trade, for example, is constructed on static assumptions; time and history are excluded. International commerce, particularly in the elementary expositions, is determined largely by a country's given resource endowment; technical change is either ignored or introduced into the model in an *ad hoc* manner.[2] In other words, most contemporary economists argue that commodity flows are determined not by differences in knowledge, technology or production functions but by differences in the relative availability of the primary factors of production, notably undifferentiated labour and homogeneous capital.[3]

Writers of a second, rather small, body of literature argue that population growth is the major stimulus to economic change and rising income per head. [4] Lastly, there are the growth theorists, many of whom exclude technical change from their models (or introduce it in an *ad hoc* manner) and attribute rising *per capita* income largely to capital accumulation and a rise in the capital – labour ratio. [5]

I. THE LOCUS OF RESEARCH EXPENDITURE

The view we shall adopt is that neither differences in resource endowment nor differences in the rate of growth of capital or labour can account for observed differences in rates of growth of income per head or for the general behaviour of the international economy. We shall argue that it is the growth and accumulation of useful knowledge, and the transformation of knowledge into final output via technical innovation, upon which the performance of the world capitalist economy ultimately depends.

One of the distinctive features of the international economy is the uneven geographical incidence of expenditure to acquire new knowledge. Most spending on research occurs in rich countries; very little is spent in poor countries. Indeed, the United Nations has estimated that 98 per cent of all expenditure on research and development in the non-socialist countries takes place in rich nations, and 70 per cent occurs in the United States alone. Only two per cent of research and development expenditure is located in underdeveloped countries. [6] That is, the rich countries spend on research, in absolute terms, 49 times as much as the poor, and in *per capita* terms they spend nearly 135 times as much. This is not surprising, perhaps, given that research expenditure is a form of investment; it is simply another manifestation of the differences which separate rich from poor countries.

The locus of research, however, is not a matter of indifference to the underdeveloped countries, since this is likely to affect (i) the types of problems to be investigated, (ii) the nature of the solution, and (iii) the groups who will benefit most directly. Agricultural research conducted in the United States, for instance, may well be concerned with economising on scarce and expensive labour, in temperate climates, by designing improved mechanical implements capable of being financed and operated by large, prosperous farmers. This research is unlikely to be of use to small and impoverished peasant cultivators in the labour-abundant tropics. Indeed one can go further. Much (but not all) of the research undertaken in the rich countries is likely to be, at best, irrelevant and, at worst, harmful to the poor countries.[7] Some of the research undertaken in the rich countries will, of course, be useful elsewhere, directly or indirectly. For example, research in the rich countries on mining techniques, methods of detecting oil or reducing the size of transistors may be directly applicable in poor countries and suitable for their conditions. Alternatively, the development of new products or techniques in rich countries, whether or not they are suitable for poor countries, may stimulate demand for commodities produced by them. The development of the motorcar, for instance, led to an enormous expansion in the demand for rubber and oil.

Over half the research conducted in the rich capitalist countries, however, is clearly of no immediate relevance to the development prospects of poor countries. Under this heading we include research on defence and space (which accounts for 46 per cent of rich-countries' research), atomic energy (over 7 per cent) and supersonic aircraft. In the long run, of course, some of this research may be harmful to the poor countries, e.g. research on weaponry. The fact that, say, arms are imported by underdeveloped countries tells us nothing meaningful about the 'gains from trade': the arms may merely facilitate destructive international conflict or internal repression of the mass of the population.[8]

Of the remaining research conducted in rich countries an unknown amount is directly prejudicial to the interests of at least some poor countries. Research on sugarbeet, for instance, has gradually reduced the cost of obtaining sugar from this temperate-climate crop. Costs have now fallen sufficiently for the cheapest sugarbeet to be fully competitive (without tariff protection) with the marginal cane grown in the tropics. As research continues one can confidently predict that the share of the world market supplied by cane producers will gradually contract. Similar phenomena will occur (and are occurring) with other products. Natural textile fibres are being replaced by synthetic fibres, as in the case of cotton and silk. Jute sacking is being replaced by plastic bags. Natural rubber has lost a large portion of the international market to synthetics, etc. In other words, research in rich countries sometimes results in augmented competition for products largely produced in poor countries. Of course the consumers in poor countries of these synthetic products and of imported substitutes for domestically produced goods may benefit—and perhaps substantially—from lower prices, but the producers in underdeveloped countries lose, whereas in the rich countries both producers and consumers gain. Even if, in the poor countries, the losses to producers are less than the gains to consumers, so that on the whole, ignoring changes in income distribution, we may say that there has been a net increase in welfare, this increase is likely to be relatively smaller than the corresponding increase in welfare in the rich countries. The fruits of greater knowledge are unequally distributed.

Moreover, it is possible to argue, following Streeten,[9] that the overwhelmingly dominant position of the rich countries in world research often results in the little research undertaken in poor countries being misdirected. Methods of investigation are established and learned in the rich countries. Standards of scientific acceptability are set in the developed countries, where, for example, expensive equipment permitting precision measurements are readily available. Even topics suitable for research may be strongly influenced by the practices followed in the rich countries. India, for example, conducts research on atomic energy while most households use animal dung as the major source of fuel. Even if the attractions of research institutions in the rich countries do not lead to an external brain drain from the poor, by inducing the acceptance of inappropriate standards, techniques and topics, they may lead in effect to an internal brain drain.

II.   TECHNICAL CHANGE AS A SOURCE OF GROWTH

A direct connection between expenditure on research and economic growth cannot be established. What can be shown, however, is that the results of econometric investigation into the sources of growth are consistent with the view that most of the growth in poor countries is due to an accumulation of capital and expansion of the labour force, whilst most of the growth in rich countries is due to an increase in factor productivity, i.e. technical change broadly interpreted. In other words, the sources of growth in the so-called Third World appear to be quite different, in terms of their relative importance, from those of the developed capitalist world. The former appears to depend for its growth largely upon an increase in the primary factors of production, whereas the latter appears to rely to a considerable degree upon an increase in the productivity of the factors of production.

Evidence from 34 countries is summarised in Table 1. It can be seen at a glance that the proportion of the growth in output attributable to the residual, which is interpreted as growth in factor productivity, is much higher in rich countries than in poor. The unweighted arithmetic average

TABLE 1. The proportion of the growth in output attributable to growth in factor productivity

Underdeveloped Countries

Latin America, 1955–64
Argentina	−43
Brazil	26
Chile	13
Colombia	22
Mexico	40
Peru, 1950–65	18
Venezuela, 1950–65	−16

Africa, 1950–65
Egypt	21
Ghana	− 7

South Asia, 1950–65
India	−34
Pakistan (East and West)	4
Sri Lanka	− 6

East Asia, 1950–65
Malaya	−10
Philippines	1
South Korea	18
Taiwan	39
Thailand	3

Europe, 1950–65
Greece	35
Spain	33
Turkey	18
Yugoslavia	8

Developed Countries, 1950–62

Belgium	63
Canada, 1949–59	16
Denmark	55
France	75
Germany	62
Israel, 1952–8	40
Italy	72
Japan, 1950–8	38
Netherlands	60
Norway	70
Sweden, 1949–59	73
United Kingdom	52
USA	41

Source: Developed countries other than Canada, Israel, Japan and Sweden: E. F. Denison, 'Economic growth', in R. E. Caves and Associates, *Britain's Economic Prospects* (Washington: Brookings Institution, 1968) Ch. 6;   these plus Argentina, Brazil, Chile, Colombia and Mexico: H. Bruton, 'Productivity growth in Latin America', *American Economic Review* (Dec. 1967);   all other countries: A. Madison, *Economic Progress and Policy in Developing Countries* (London: Allen and Unwin, 1970) Ch. 2.

for the 21 underdeveloped countries is only 9 per cent, while the average for the 13 developed countries is 55 per cent.

It would be rash to accept the figures in the table uncritically. Most of them were obtained from econometric estimates of equations of the following type:[10]

$$g = ak + (1 - a)n + r$$

where g = rate of growth of output,
  k = rate of growth of the stock of capital,
  n = rate of growth of the labour force,
  r = a residual attributed to technical change, i.e. growth in
    total factor productivity, and
  a and $(1 - a)$ are weights.

There are several strong criticisms which can be made of this method of estimating the sources of growth.[11] Indeed, some would argue that the whole approach is conceptually so dubious that it ought to be abandoned. In my opinion this is an extreme position, but the inherent and practical weaknesses of the approach should not be ignored. The estimating equation may not accurately reflect the relationship between inputs of capital and labour and the resulting flow of output. For example, the weights may not sum to unity. Alternatively, the growth of capital k and technical change r may be interdependent rather than independent sources of growth as the equation implies. The identification of the residual with technical change may not be entirely persuasive.[12] Lastly, the quality of the basic data underlying the estimates may be unreliable. Indeed the negative value for the residual that is occasionally obtained is a clear warning of unreliability.

The countries included in Table 1 represent a non-random sample. The period covered is not uniform. The results are taken from studies conducted by three different authors who used different methods of estimation. Notwithstanding these shortcomings, however, the differences between the two groups of countries are so dramatic that it is highly improbable that our general conclusion will be disproved by subsequent empirical work. Technical change may not be precisely 6 times more important as a source of growth in rich countries than in poor, as the table suggests, but there can be little doubt that this is the correct order of magnitude.

The data available are not conclusive, but they are consistent with what we know from common sense. The data are sufficient to establish that most expenditure to acquire new knowledge is concentrated in a small number of highly developed countries and that these countries do in fact enjoy rapid rates of technological innovation. Furthermore, it is likely that the pattern of technical change helps to perpetuate international inequality in the distribution of income. This arises from three biases: the locational bias of innovation in favour of rich countries; a commodity bias against the crops and raw materials produced in poor countries; and a factor bias against labour, the relatively abundant factor in most underdeveloped countries. Technical change in practice often tends to reduce the prices of some primary commodities and of labour below what they would otherwise have been and, consequently, to dampen the rate of growth of national income of labour-abundant, primary-producing countries.[13] It is not inevitable that technical changes have this result, but as long as they are a virtual monopoly of rich countries it seems probable that they will.

III. ASYMMETRIES IN INTERNATIONAL ECONOMIC RELATIONS

International economic intercourse is characterised by a series of asymmetries of which four are relevant to the present discussion. First, many rich countries are large in terms of population and gross national product, whereas most (but not all) poor countries are small. For example, well over half the underdeveloped countries of the world have less than 5 million inhabitants; in contrast, only seven rich countries are this small.[14] On the other hand, most of the people in underdeveloped countries live in a few very large countries: India, Indonesia, Bangladesh, etc.

Secondly, the many poor countries which are small are heavily dependent on international trade, yet their exports account for a tiny fraction of world commerce.[15] The large, rich countries, on the other hand, are much less dependent on trade, yet account for a large proportion of it. The most dramatic illustration is the United States, where exports account for less than five per cent of the GNP but nearly 16 per cent of total world trade. The US depends relatively little on its trading partners whereas the rest of the world depends a great deal on the US. In Malta, exports represent almost half the GNP; in Malaysia, 45 per cent; in Libya, two-thirds; in Sri Lanka, 21 per cent. Yet Sri Lanka's exports, for instance, account for only 0.15 per cent of world trade.

Thirdly, the mass of small, underdeveloped countries are confronted by large, highly developed companies. Many international corporations control resources which exceed the national income of most poor countries. The annual sales of General Motors, for example, are greater than the GNP of all underdeveloped countries except China and India. Indeed, the wealth (a stock) of some individuals is greater than the income (a flow) of some countries. The two richest Americans, for instance, are each worth about $1,500 million. This is greater than the national income of Kenya and nearly as much as that of Uruguay. In fact, nearly half the underdeveloped countries have a GNP which is smaller than the assets of the late J. Paul Getty.

Strictly speaking, of course, it is not appropriate to compare the gross output of companies with the net output of countries, or the stock of assets of persons with the flow of national income generated by a stock. The basic point we are making, however, is that corporate and personal wealth confer power. Vertically-integrated corporations, through their transfer-pricing policies, can avoid taxation and thereby affect the ability of a poor country to mobilise resources for economic development.[16] The export policies of individual firms virtually determine the amount of foreign exchange available to some countries. These 'company countries' and 'banana republics' have very little capacity for independent action. In many underdeveloped countries, apart from the oil-producing nations, the bargaining strength of some foreign corporations is substantially greater than that of the local government. Furthermore, the increasing strength of the international corporations may ultimately erode the nation-state system. This point is ably presented by Hymer and Rowthorn:

> . . . it is clear that the growth of multinational corporations, by itself, tends to weaken nation-states. Multinational corporations render ineffective many traditional policy instruments, the capacity to tax, to restrict credit, to plan investment, etc., because of their international flexibility. In addition, multinational corporations act as a vehicle for the intrusion of the policies of one country into another with the ultimate effect of lessening the power of both.[17]

The power of the multinational firm has become apparent even in the rich countries of Western Europe. The pronouncements of Henry Ford II on the British economy make television news and front-page headlines. Even so, for the French to worry about 'The American Challenge' may seem slightly absurd, but for a country like Chile to ignore it would be foolish, as the ITT affair and similar episodes throughout history demonstrate.

Finally, there is technical change, the phenomenon with which we are primarily concerned. The development of new products and new techniques of production has increased the flexibility of the industrial economies and, as we have seen, become the major cause of the acceleration in the rate of growth that has occurred in the last quarter of a century. Knowledge has been generated in the rich, capital-abundant countries, and this has improved their performance and increased their political and economic power. The poor countries, on the other hand, have usually responded passively to technical change originating abroad.[18] The development of new products and techniques has sometimes dislocated their economies and we shall argue below that in some cases it has increased their rigidity and lowered the rate of growth.

The most widely accepted theories of international trade would lead one to believe that the free flow of commodities and factors of production would tend to reduce international inequality and accelerate the growth of the most backward economies. There is no evidence, however, that this has happened. Beckerman and Bacon report that the poorest 10 per cent of the world's population account for only 1.6 per cent of world consumption, and the bottom 30 per cent of the population account for only 10.4 per cent. The richest 10 per cent, in contrast, account for over 35 per cent of total world consumption.[19] They conclude that 'the international size distribution of income is probably far more unequal than the distribution *within* any developed country',[20] and, moreover, there is no tendency for inequality to diminish.

The poor countries, then, tend to be a mixture of small, weak, specialised[21] and highly dependent economies. They confront a set of large, powerful, diversified economies which have the capacity to generate their own sources of growth. The rich countries, that is, initiate change and the poor countries largely respond to it as best they can.

IV. DISTRIBUTION OF THE GAINS FROM TRADE

Granted, then, that the underdeveloped countries are highly specialised producers and have fully participated in the international division of labour, the question as to whether and by how much they have gained from trade arises. The most widely accepted answer is presented in terms of production frontiers and community indifferent curves. Assuming full employment, perfect competition, resource mobility and factor-price flexibility it can be shown that trade leads to greater specialisation and higher welfare and income. Furthermore, if the economy is growing, the static gains from trade will be compounded. Better still, the higher level of income may be associated with a higher rate of saving and investment and, hence, a faster rate of growth.[22]

If, however, resources are immobile, both the static and dynamic gains from trade will be greatly reduced, because the gains from trade arise in large part from the ability of an economy to reallocate resources towards those sectors which experience a comparative advantage. If reallocation is impossible, i.e. if the economy has a 'transformation problem', many of the advantages of free international trade disappear. Unfortunately, resources *are* relatively immobile in many underdeveloped countries.[23]

There are several reasons for this. First, the natural resource endowment may be limited. Small countries are unlikely to have diversified resources and hence will find it difficult to alter the sectoral composition of production in response to changes in relative prices. Secondly, widespread illiteracy and a generally poor educational system means that labour cannot readily be shifted from one sector to another. It is very difficult and costly, for example, to convert an illiterate semi-subsistence farmer into a skilled machine-tool operator, although it is possible, of course, for a farmer to switch from, say, jute to rice production. Thirdly, capital may also be immobile. This will occur if most capital is fixed capital and is specific to a particular activity. For example, a petroleum refinery cannot be converted into a cement plant, or a palm-oil plantation into a herd of livestock. In fact, the mobility of capital largely depends on the rate of investment; the greater the additions to the stock of capital, the easier it is to alter the composition of the stock of capital. In other words, the ability to reallocate resources depends in part upon the rate of growth, which in turn is linked to the rate of technical change. Growth provides flexibility and enables a country to respond quickly to changing opportunities. Thus the rich, rapidly expanding countries are able to benefit from the opportunity to trade, while the poor, slowly growing countries are not, or at least not to the same extent.

The problems of adjustment are accentuated if to resource immobility is added downward factor-price rigidity. In this case not only will output not expand in the sector which enjoys a comparative advantage, but the sector which suffers from a comparative disadvantage—perhaps as a result of technical change abroad—will actually contract, and thus the level of income and employment will fall. Free trade, far from raising economic welfare, may lower it.

This point has been forcefully stated by Lord Balogh:

> If the effects of accumulation and increasing returns are excluded by assumption from the traditional approach, so is the related problem of *technical progress*. . . . The model . . . suggests a principle of symmetry whereby the impact of . . . a limited (once-for-all technical) change is random or unbiased. No doubt it is admitted that some countries or areas *could* be hurt by change; but the impression most insistently conveyed is that this would be the exception rather than the rule. No emphasis is laid on the continuity of the process and on its close connexion with capital accumulation. Thus the consequential disturbance of the comparative advantage of the poorer areas, which have to rely for their exports on primary products produced by primitive methods, is disregarded.[24]

Moreover, it is stressed that 'in a framework of disparate economic growth . . . technical progress seems not merely to have increased disparities historically, but to have acted as a positive impediment to the development of the poorer areas'.[25]

Historically, there is little doubt that international trade has created underdevelopment as well as facilitated development. Those who lost from international trade tried to avoid it, while those who gained often used force of arms to compel its continuation. Many writers, in fact, have noted the association of colonialism and imperialism with the expansion of foreign commerce and overseas investment. Some have argued, rather paradoxically, that force must sometimes be used to encourage colonial peoples to participate in the long-run mutual benefits of international trade,[26] but the more straightforward interpretation is that the commercial penetration of Europe into Latin America, Asia and Africa was often at the expense of the well-being of the majority of the colonised peoples. It goes against one's common sense to argue that imperialism was necessary because people did not know that free trade was good for them.

Moreover, if the expansion of trade is accompanied by technical change, as it often was in the past and certainly is today, the consequences for poor and inflexible economies can be severe. Technical change, after all, reduces the demand for certain commodities and certain factors of production, at least in the short run. If the factors so released are unable to find employment elsewhere, the net effect of an innovation may be to reduce rather than to raise welfare. The likelihood of technical change reducing welfare is greater in countries where resources are immobile and growth is slow, i.e. in underdeveloped countries. Even as ardent a free trader as Sir John Hicks accepts this. He notes that

> . . . the labour that is thrown out (as a result of technical change) may be in one country, and the expansion in demand for labour, which is the effect of the accumulation of capital that results, may be in another. The English handloom weavers, who were displaced by textile machinery, would (in the end and after much travail) find re-employment in England; but what of the Indian weavers who were displaced by the same improvement? Even in their case there would be a favourable effect, somewhere; but it might be anywhere; there would be no particular reason why it should be in India. The poorer the country, the narrower will be its range of opportunities; the more likely, therefore, it is that it will suffer long-lasting damage, now and then, from a backwash of improvements that have occurred elsewhere.[27]

V. DYNAMIC ASPECTS OF COMPARATIVE ADVANTAGE

Evidently comparative advantage is not a static phenomenon and no one would wish to argue literally that it is. Many writers, however, have strongly implied that it changes rather slowly and essentially randomly. Our view, in contrast, is that comparative advantage can and does change swiftly, particularly as a result of technological developments, and that it tends to change systematically in favour of rich countries. That is, the double factoral terms of trade tend to move persistently in favour of the rich countries. The basic reason for this is that exports from rich countries, and especially the rapidly expanding exporting sectors, are intensive in knowledge and advanced technology.[28]

Compared to the underdeveloped countries, a large proportion of technically trained personnel in the rich countries are employed in industry, particularly manufacturing. Furthermore, these people are engaged not only in production but also in applied research and development and in management. It is noteworthy that 74 per cent of the scientists and engineers in the United States are employed in industry.[29] Many of the remainder are employed by government or the universities and are occupied in tasks which directly or indirectly increase the flow of technical change.

Research in the rich countries is highly concentrated on a few

branches of industry and, indeed, within a relatively few firms. The OECD reports that 76.1 per cent of total research and development expenditure in US manufacturing in 1963–4 was accounted for by three sectors: aircraft (38.3 per cent), electronics (24.8 per cent) and chemicals (13.0 per cent). The eight largest firms (by size of their R & D programmes) accounted for 35 per cent of total industrial expenditure on research and development, and the 40 largest firms for 70 per cent.[30] The intense concentration of research effort in the rich countries can be viewed in yet another way. Five industries in the United States in 1962 accounted for 89.4 per cent of US industrial research and development expenditure. These same industries accounted for 39.1 per cent of total US sales of manufactured goods and 72 per cent of US exports of manufactured goods.[31] In other words, not only does spending on research centre on the rich countries, but within the rich countries research is concentrated on a few industries which account for a disproportionate amount of the exports from rich countries.

The evidence, although not conclusive, is consistent with the hypothesis that a major determinant of changes in the pattern of world trade is the level and composition of spending on research and innovation in the developed countries. If this view turns out to be correct, it follows that most underdeveloped countries are confined to passively adapting as best they can to continuous dynamic processes originating elsewhere. Some countries, for reasons explained above, may be able to adapt less readily than others. Moreover, the failure to adapt may be more serious for some countries than others, depending upon the nature and extent of their dependence on foreign trade. All poor countries, however, face a permanent threat to their trading position because of the capacity of the developed countries (given time and effort) to produce commodities that are competitive with the exports of underdeveloped countries.

None the less, at any given moment the physical items exchanged through trade are likely to reflect comparative advantage.[32] It does not follow, however, that there is an equal exchange of value. Equal or equivalent exchange would occur only if perfect competition prevailed world-wide and there were no discrepancies between private and social values, so that the price of all commodities corresponded to the social marginal cost of production. I do not wish to imply that such a situation would necessarily be desirable. The distribution of income, for example, might be quite unacceptable. Equivalent exchange merely implies that the world economy is in a Pareto optimum and hence that there are no monopoly rents. One of the implications of the theory we have been developing, however, is that perfect competition cannot prevail even if it existed initially. The concentration of technical change in a few countries, industries and firms constantly re-creates a monopolistic organisation of industry and enables innovating enterprises to price their products in such a way as to include a substantial element of rent. The rent element in prices, in turn, ensures that value exchanged through trade will favour the rich countries (where innovation occurs) and prejudice the development of poor countries (whose exports, frequently but not always, are sold on competitive markets).[33]

It has been emphasised by Sanjaya Lall, quite rightly, that the problem of unequal exchange is especially likely to arise in the case of new products traded in uncompetitive markets organised by multinational corporations.[34] Precisely in these instances are prices not determined by competitive forces but by the pricing policy of large monopolistic enterprises. The multinational corporations are in a strong position to extract part of the surplus from underdeveloped countries, in the form of a rent on technology, bcause of their vertically-integrated operations.

It is, perhaps, not widely known that approximately one-third of total US foreign trade in manufactured products in 1970 was intra-firm trade. Moreover, the relative importance of intra-firm trade is rising. In other words, arms-length trading in more-or-less competitive markets is of declining significance in international commerce. The acceleration of the pace of technical change in the industrial nations has been accompanied by changes in marketing and production arrangements—notably, with greater emphasis on sales through overseas subsidiaries rather than by direct exporting and on vertical integration—which have enabled the innovating firms and countries to retain for themselves the benefits of technological improvements rather than distribute them equitably throughout the world. Falling costs of manufacturing have been associated with higher factor payments in a minority of countries rather than lower prices in all countries. Thus even when research conducted in rich countries is potentially of direct benefit to the poor, the potential benefits are not (or are not fully) translated into actual benefits because of the mechanism of unequal exchange, namely, the pricing policies of multinational enterprises.

VI. FLOWS OF SKILLED MANPOWER

International inequality is transmitted not only by commodity flows but also by movements of factors of production. This is an unorthodox position. The more common view is that factors of production would move from countries where they are abundant (and hence poorly remunerated) to countries where they are scarce (and hence well rewarded). The usual presumption is that if factors were free to move, capital and skilled labour would migrate from the developed to the underdeveloped countries while unskilled labour would emigrate from the poor countries to the rich. This process would continue until the return on capital and the reward to labour were the same in all countries, and in the course of this 'factor-price equalisation' inequality would tend to diminish.

The concentration of rapid technical change in a few countries, however, invalidates the orthodox analysis. The effect of technical change is continuously to raise factor productivities, the level of income and rates of growth in the rich countries. This acts as a cumulatively disequilibrating phenomenon, the result of which is that the technologically progressive countries tend to attract all mobile scarce resources from the underdeveloped countries.[35] On balance, savings and skilled personnel flow not from rich to poor countries but from poor to rich. In the process, international inequality is increased and underdevelopment is accentuated.

The so-called brain drain is a case in point. Wages and salaries of doctors, scientists and engineers in the developed countries are a multiple of what they are in underdeveloped countries, despite the fact that these skills are far more abundant in the former. The income differential induces international migration, and this has the effect of reducing supplies of skilled personnel in countries where they are scarce and increasing supplies where already they are abundant.

The United States alone attracts several thousand professionally qualified personnel a year from the underdeveloped countries, as the data in Table 2 indicate. Additional thousands are attracted to the major European nations: Germany, France and the United Kingdom.

The outflow of professional manpower from poor to rich countries has several effects. First, it obviously raises the income of the migrants. Secondly, if the outflow is more than of marginal significance, it reduces

TABLE 2. Immigration of professional manpower from underdeveloped countries into the United States, 1962–9

Doctors, dentists and surgeons	12,805
Natural scientists	6,528
Social scientists	1,674
Engineers	19,358

Source: J. Bhagwati and W. Dellafar, 'The brain drain and income taxation', *World Development* (Feb. 1973) p. 98, Table 1.

the economic surplus (and hence income) of the remaining persons in the underdeveloped country. Thirdly, it tends to raise the wages of the remaining professional manpower in underdeveloped countries. (In the limiting case these wages would rise to the levels encountered in the developed countries.) This implies, fourthly, that income within the underdeveloped country will become more unequal, thereby further reducing the standard of living of non-professional people, i.e. of the poor. This in turn, fifthly, may undermine the social cohesion of the nation and result in greater domestic strife.

Some of these effects can be illustrated diagrammatically in Figure 2. Assume initially there were N_1 professional personnel in an under-developed country receiving a wage of W_1, equivalent to their marginal social product. If N_2N_1 people migrate, national income will fall by AN_2N_1C, of which BN_2N_1C formerly was paid to the migrants. Real national income for the remaining residents therefore declines by ABC. The nation as a whole, excluding migrants, is worse off.

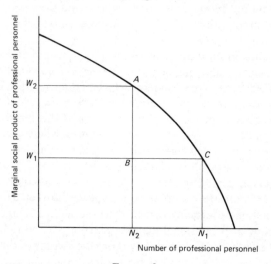

FIGURE 2

The wage of the remaining N_2 professionals, however, rises to W_2. Thus income inequality increases. Moreover, since there has been no over-all improvement in productive efficiency, the rise in income of the professional classes must be at the expense of the non-professional classes, i.e. of the mass of the population. Figure 2 indicates that wages received by the remaining professionals increases by a total amount equivalent to W_1W_2AB. This is also equivalent to the loss incurred by non-professionals, arising from the change in the distribution of income. In other words, there are two components to the losses inflicted on the non-professional classes: an income effect (*ABC*) and a distribution effect (*W₁W₂AB*). The total loss is the sum of these two: $W_1 W_2 AC$.

VII. THE MIGRATION OF FINANCE CAPITAL

The brain drain has become recognized as an important feature of the contemporary world economy. What has not become recognised, however, is that a similar analysis to that of the previous section applies to international movements of finance capital. Indeed there are many myths about the role of flows of foreign private capital into the underdeveloped countries.

Most direct overseas investment in poor countries is channelled not into primary activities such as petroleum but into the manufacturing sector. In Latin America, for example, the share of US direct private investment in manufacturing rose from 10.7 per cent of total US direct investment in the region in 1957 to 60.5 per cent in 1967. Furthermore, despite this dramatic change in the composition of overseas investment in the Third World, there is no evidence that direct investment as a whole is increasing rapidly. On the contrary, the amount of capital received by poor countries from the rich is derisory, as is clear from Table 3.

TABLE 3. US direct manufacturing investment abroad, 1971

	Amount ($ 10⁶)	Proportion (% of total)
Developed countries	29,483	83
Underdeveloped countries	5,991	17
TOTAL	35,475	100

Source: US Department of Commerce, *Survey of Current Business* (Nov. 1972).

In 1971 the United States invested directly in manufacturing less than $6,000 million in the poor countries. This was equivalent to only 17 per cent of total investment abroad in the manufacturing sector in that year. Moreover, within the Third World, most US investment went to the less poor areas. Specifically, in 1971 nearly 83 per cent (i.e. $4,998 million) of US direct investment in the manufacturing sector in underdeveloped countries was located in Latin America. Less than $1,000 million was available for the whole of Asia and Africa, both of which regions are poorer and more populous than Latin America. A broadly similar pattern is characteristic of British direct investment: in 1971 less than 12 per cent of direct investment (not including portfolio investment and investment by oil companies) was located in underdeveloped countries: the remaining 88 per cent was in rich countries.[36]

The explanation for the concentration of foreign investment in rich countries is that in general the return on investment in the rich, capital-abundant countries is higher than in the poor, capital-scarce countries. This goes contrary to a widely accepted view but seems to be supported by the available data. Conventional theory predicts that profit rates in underdeveloped countries would be substantially greater than in developed economies and this, in turn, would lead to a large flow of savings (or finance capital) from the latter to the former. When it is observed that savings flow from poor countries to rich, the conventional theorist is reduced to mumbling something about political uncertainty, capital flight and risk. In our opinion, however, one should naturally expect that capital would flow toward the rich countries, where, as a result of continuous technical change and innovation, profit rates are relatively high.[37] The fragmentary information at hand is at least consistent with this approach.

We have seen that most US direct investment in underdeveloped countries is in Latin America. Yet the data in Table 4 indicate that the return on this investment is lower than the return in any developed region except Canada—despite tariffs, quota restrictions, tax exemptions, subsidies, etc., which are designed to increase the profitability of investment in Latin America. Of course, the data are not completely

TABLE 4. Rate of profit on US private overseas investment, average 1965–70

Country	Profit rate (%)	
	Manufacturing	Other industries
Japan	21.8	17.2
UK	14.4	12.6
EEC	12.1	7.8
Other Western Europe	10.6	17.6
Australia, New Zealand and South Africa	11.0	12.7
Canada	7.8	6.8
Latin America	9.9	7.7
Other underdeveloped areas	11.5	10.9

Source: US Department of Commerce, *Survey of Current Business* (Oct. 1971).

satisfactory. The figures in the table are average rates of return, not the marginal rates that are strictly necessary to test our (and the neoclassical) hypothesis.[38] Moreover, risk is ignored, as are profits arising from transfer-pricing. None the less, it seems reasonable to conclude that the return on investment may well be higher in rich countries than in poor and this may explain why most foreign investment is by one rich country in another.

The higher rates of profit obtainable in the developed countries, however, also tend to attract savings and finance capital from the underdeveloped countries. That is, there are strong forces in the world economy which operate in such a way that the poor countries tend to be deprived of their relatively meagre savings by the rich.[39] This, evidently, helps to perpetuate and accentuate inequality at the world level. This polarisation of the international economy (and indeed of regions within a national economy) is a cumulative process arising from the location and nature of technical change and is an integral feature of the operation of a capitalist economic system.

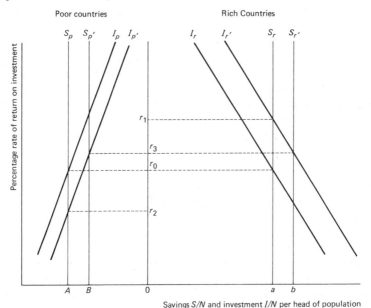

FIGURE 3

Some insight into how the system works can be obtained from a simple diagram (Figure 3). On the horizontal axis we measure flows of savings and investment per head for a poor and for a rich country. On the vertical axis we measure the percentage rate of return on investment. We assume that the returns on savings are equal to those on investment, i.e. costs of intermediation are ignored.

Initially the world economy is in equilibrium. The profit rate on investment is the same in both the poor and rich country (r_0) and, therefore, there is no tendency for savings to move in either direction. Investment per head in each country depends entirely on the amount of savings undertaken in that country. The amount saved, in turn, is assumed for simplicity to be independent of the rate of return, although in which country the savings are placed does depend on the rate of return.

Imagine now that research and development in the rich countries leads to technical change such that the investment schedule I_r shifts outward and to the right, say, to I_r'. The rate of return on investment in the rich country then rises from r_0 to r_1. As we have seen, technical change in a rich country may be biased against products produced in poor countries. If this occurs, the profitability of investment in poor countries will decline; the investment schedule may shift inwards from I_p to I_p', thereby reducing the profit rate from r_0 to r_2.

Where once the return on investment was identical in rich countries and poor, now there is a large differential between r_2 and r_1, as a result of technical change. This differential constitutes a disequilibrium situation and a strong tendency will emerge for the differential to be closed by a movement of savings and finance capital from the poor country to the rich. In terms of Figure 3, AB savings will flow from the poor country to the rich. This can be represented by a shift of S_p to S_p' and by an equal shift of S_r to S_r'. (Note that $ab = AB$.) The return on investment in the poor country will rise from r_2 to r_3, while the return in the rich country will fall from r_1 to r_3. In practice, of course, equilibrium is unlikely ever to be achieved because technical change (and other phenomena) continuously disturb the system. In other words, one should expect a persistent tendency for investible resources to flow towards the developed countries.

This flow of resources is in the reverse direction to that predicted by most economic analysis. It tends to increase international inequality, not diminish it. Moreover, the effects of the resource flows are asymmetrical. The inflow of resources from the underdeveloped country represents a small fraction of total investment per head in the rich, whereas the outflow of resources may represent a substantial proportion of the *per capita* economic surplus available for investment in the poor country. That is, inflows contribute only marginally to increasing the prosperity of the developed countries, but unless they are stopped they can contribute mightily to perpetuating poverty in the underdeveloped countries.[40] In terms of our diagram,

$$|ab/0b| < |AB/A0|$$

Lastly, as we have seen, the transfer of savings from the poor to the rich country raises the return on capital in the former. This change in factor payments alters the distribution of income within the underdeveloped country in favour of the capitalist class. In other words, the poorest (non-property-owning) people in poor countries suffer doubly. They lose partly because a portion of the investible surplus is siphoned off to the rich countries and partly because the remaining income is redistributed against them. International capital movements, like the migration of professional manpower, tend to depress the *per capita* income of underdeveloped countries and to contribute towards its unequal distribution.

VIII. DIRECT INVESTMENT

The analysis of the previous section was in terms of the geographical mobility of savings and finance capital. Direct overseas investment by multinational corporations was not considered. Our argument was that the return on investment was higher in rich countries than in poor and that in consequence savings would tend to leave the underdeveloped countries in search of higher earnings elsewhere. The high return on investment, however, was due not to a shortage of capital in rich countries but to the presence there of a steady flow of new products and new techniques which creates investment opportunities.

The implication of this is that the profits from investing in rich countries reflect, at least in part, a monopoly rent arising from the possession of knowledge. More generally, the effect of the creation of new knowledge in rich countries is to raise the return on capital invested by citizens and firms of rich countries, whether or not the capital is invested in a rich or in a poor country.

A commercial institution in a developed country which wants to exploit an innovation can do so in a variety of ways: by producing at home and exporting abroad; by direct investment overseas; by selling patent rights and licences, etc. Many factors will determine which of these devices is used and it is beyond the scope of this chapter to examine the alternatives in detail. If our general analysis is correct, however, one would expect that when multinational corporations do invest in

34   *International Inequality and National Poverty*

underdeveloped countries they will obtain a higher rate of return than local capitalists: the payments received by foreigners are not for capital as such but for knowledge, a scarce and monopolised factor of production.

Unfortunately, only fragmentary evidence is available with which to test our hypothesis. Such data as exist, however, provide some support for our view. A study in India, for example, indicated that a sample of 366 foreign-controlled companies enjoyed a profit rate nearly 50 per cent higher than a sample of 1,944 Indian-controlled companies.

TABLE 5. India: Gross profits on total capital employed, average 1966/7 – 1967/8 (percentage)

1,944 Indian-controlled companies	8.0
366 Foreign-controlled companies	11.8

Source: Prabhat Patnaik, *Private corporate industrial investment in India, 1947–67: Factors affecting its size, cyclical fluctuation and sectoral distribution*, D. Phil. thesis, Oxford University, 1973, Table 4.6, p. 134; citing *Reserve Bank of India Bulletin* (June 1970 and May 1972).
Note: Profits are before tax but after depreciation.

TABLE 6. Profit rates of 53 foreign-owned manufacturing firms in Colombia average 1966–70

	Concept	*Profit Rate*
(1)	Declared profits after tax as per cent of net worth	8.4
(2)	Declared profits after tax plus royalty payments as per cent of net worth	13.1
(3)	Declared profits after tax plus royalties plus overpricing of intra-firm imports as per cent of net worth	52.0
(4)	Profits before tax plus royalties plus interest payments as per cent of net worth plus long-term loans plus bank loans	9.3
(5)	Profits before tax plus royalties plus interest payments as per cent of net worth plus long-term loans plus short-term credit	2.2

Source: Daniel Chudnovsky, *Foreign manufacturing firms' behaviour in Colombia: A study of the influence of technology, advertising and financing upon profitability, 1966–70*, D. Phil. thesis, Oxford University, 1973, Ch. III.
Note: The estimate for concept (3) is based on data from 13 firms only, of which 10 were pharmaceutical enterprises.

The source of profits of foreign-owned corporations emerges quite clearly from data collected in Colombia and reproduced in Table 6. The after-tax profit rate of 53 foreign manufacturing enterprises varied from 8.4 to 52.0 per cent of net worth, depending on whether or not royalty payments and earnings from intra-firm sales were included in the numerator. The payment to foreign capital as such was negligible in comparison to the amount earned from royalties and intra-firm sales. Moreover, and this is a crucial point, the profits on total capital employed, i.e. net worth plus long- and short-term loans, was very low, perhaps as low as 2.2 per cent.[41]

Some foreign-owned manufacturing firms earned a great deal of money in Colombia not by providing capital to a capital-scarce economy but by reaping monopoly rents on knowledge generated in the developed countries. The return on Colombian capital supplied to the 53 manufacturing firms was low (in some cases the real rate of interest was negative), whereas the return on foreign technology supplied to the 53 firms was exceptionally high. As a result, most of the value-added produced by the firms accrued to foreigners and the Colombian economy benefited little. In fact, in some cases where protection was heavy the amount received by foreigners may have exceeded real value-added, i.e. the value-added obtained when all outputs and material inputs are valued at their social opportunity cost. In such cases Colombia would have lost absolutely.

IX. SUMMARY

There has been a revival of theories which explain how international economic intercourse may be relatively or absolutely harmful to some of the participating countries. All these theories—despite their differences of emphasis, of method and even of the basic questions which are posed—share one thing in common: their point of departure is that the world is characterised by a conflict of interests. The usual assumption of many economists is that a harmony of interests prevails in economic relations. Thus there is no need for an economic theory of dependency, of neo-colonialism or of imperialism; these are political, sociological and cultural phenomena, not economic.

The view expounded in this chapter, in contrast, is that in a world capitalist system composed of nation-states and characterised by rapid technical progress in the developed countries, the poor countries would tend to be deprived of their most valuable resources, namely, high-level manpower and national economic surplus. These resources are extracted in a variety of ways—through trade, through migration, through flows of finance capital—with the result that international inequality is increased and, in some cases, the standard of living of the mass of the poor is depressed absolutely. In other words, underdevelopment is accentuated. Indeed, in my opinion, underdevelopment should be understood as a product of capitalism, the consequence of an economy being deprived of its own resources. Countries can become impoverished in a variety of ways, e.g. through pillage or destruction, but they can become underdeveloped, i.e. structurally impoverished, only as a result of the operation of forces inherent in a capitalist system.

In Section I it was shown that almost all expenditure on research and technical development occurs in the rich countries and it was argued that in many instances this research is harmful to the underdeveloped countries. In Section II it was shown that growth in the rich countries, unlike that in the poor, is largely due to technical change. Again, it was suggested that the various biases which accompany this technical change, while accelerating expansion in rich countries, may retard it in the poor. Four asymmetries in international economic relations are discussed in Section III. It is claimed that these increase the dependence of the underdeveloped countries on international trade, weaken their bargaining strength and power for independent action and place them in a position of having to adapt passively to changes originating elsewhere. Adaptation, however, is often costly and in Section IV we argue that the gains from trade are so unequally distributed that in fact the underdeveloped countries have often suffered hardship as a consequence of the way they participate in international trade. The problem becomes particularly acute, as argued in Section V, when technical change in a few industries and firms in rich countries enables them to reap large monopoly rents on their technical knowledge. This phenomenon is a major cause of unequal exchange.

Inequality generated by commodity flows is exacerbated by movements of capital and labour. In Section VI was indicated the way movements of highly skilled personnel both reduce the *per capita* income of underdeveloped countries and accentuate inequality in the distribution of this lower income. A similar analysis of flows of finance capital was conducted in Section VII. It was shown that, in general, profit rates on foreign investment in manufacturing are higher in rich countries than in poor, and, as a result, savings tend to flow from capital-scarce to capital-abundant countries. This further impoverishes the underdeveloped countries and increases both national and international inequality. There is, of course, some direct investment by multinational corporations in underdeveloped countries. It is argued in Section VIII, however, that the high profit rates sometimes earned by these corporations reflect not the scarcity price of capital but a monopoly rent on knowledge produced in the developed countries. The forces tending to produce underdevelopment and perpetuate international inequality are automatic, persistent and cumulative. They do not originate from the malevolence of multinational corporations or the governments of wealthy nations. In fact the forces creating inequality are sufficiently powerful to nullify the occasional benevolent acts of individuals and institutions concerned to reduce the gulf which divides the rich from the poor. Underdevelopment and international inequality are inevitable in a system which concentrates technical advance in a few countries and allocates resources on the basis of the profit-maximising principle. It is rapid technical change which enables the rich countries to develop relatively swiftly and it is the absence of technical change which condemns the underdeveloped countries to comparative stagnation of *per capita* income.[42] It is rapid technical change and the accompanying monopoly of new knowledge which raises the productivity of labour and wages and sustains a relatively high rate of profit in the rich countries. The monopoly of advanced technology, in turn, enables the rich countries to extract super-normal profits and rents from the poor countries either through trade or, in a few cases, by direct investment. Finally, the high level of factor earnings in the rich countries enables them to deprive the poor countries of their most valuable financial and human resources through induced international migration. In these ways a part of the potential economic surplus of the poor countries is drained away to the rich countries.

NOTES AND REFERENCES

1. Joseph A. Schumpeter, *The Theory of Economic Development* (Harvard University Press, 1959) p. 64, n. 1.
2. Many of the best-known articles in this body of literature are collected together in Jagdish Bhagwati (ed.), *International Trade* (Harmondsworth: Penguin, 1969). Several references to literature which does emphasise technical change as a determinant of trade are included in Note 28.
3. Thomas Balogh has been a consistent critic of this standard trade theory. See his *Unequal Partners*, Vol. 1, Theoretical Introduction (Basil Blackwell, 1963).
4. See Ester Boserup, *The Conditions of Agricultural Growth* (London: Allen and Unwin, 1965); Colin Clark, *Population Growth and Land Use* (London:

Macmillan, 1967); Albert Hirschman, *The Strategy of Economic Development* (Yale University Press, 1958) pp. 176–82.

5. The best survey still is F. H. Hahn and R. C. O. Matthews, 'The theory of economic growth: A survey', *Economic Journal* (Dec. 1964). It is noteworthy that in this survey article, exceeding a hundred pages, only a quarter of the space was devoted to a discussion of models containing technical progress. Simon Kuznets, on the other hand, observes that 'much of the distinctive substance of modern economic growth' consists of the 'mass application of technological innovations'. See his 'Modern economic growth: Findings and reflections', *American Economic Review* (June 1973) p. 250.

6. United Nations, *Science and Technology for Development: Proposals for the Second United Nations Development Decade* (New York, 1970) p. 23.

7. This point has been stressed by Paul Streeten. See his *Frontiers of Development Studies* (London: Macmillan, 1972) Ch. 22.

8. It has been estimated that, in the 25 years since the end of the Second World War, 93 wars occurred in the Third World. See Istvan Kende, *Local Wars in Asia, Africa and Latin America, 1945–1969*, Center for Afro-Asian Research of the Hungarian Academy of Sciences (Budapest, 1972).

9. Op. cit.

10. See the pioneering article by R. M. Solow, 'Technical change and the aggregate production function', *Review of Economics and Statistics* (Aug. 1957). Subsequent developments in the literature are summarised in C. Kennedy and A. P. Thirlwall, 'Technical progress: A survey', *Economic Journal* (Mar. 1972).

11. See R. R. Nelson, 'Recent exercises in growth accounting: New understanding or dead end?', *American Economic Review* (June 1973); also see Moses Abramovitz and Paul A. David, 'Reinterpreting economic growth: Parables and realities', *American Economic Review* (May 1973).

12. The residual is in practice a composite index with unknown weights given to technical innovation narrowly defined, economies of scale and 'learning by doing'. It is not necessary for the purposes of our argument to separate these three components. It should be noted, however, that the operation of 'Verdoorn's law' implies that a faster rate of growth results in a higher residual. Thus g and r are mutually determined.

13. Our argument is not that technical innovation in rich countries necessarily has a labour-saving bias when examined from the point of view of factor proportions and relative marginal products prevailing in rich countries. It is that innovations in rich countries, when viewed from the perspective of poor countries, tend to be biased against labour. For example, an innovation of any sort in sugarbeet production is biased against labour employed in growing sugarcane.

14. New Zealand, Denmark, Finland, Norway, Ireland, Luxembourg and Iceland.

15. An exception, of course, is the relatively small number of oil-exporting countries which account for a large fraction of world trade in petroleum.

16. The literature on the multinational corporation is expanding swiftly. One of the best studies is Edith Penrose, *The Large International Firm in Developing Countries* (London: Allen and Unwin, 1968). Also of interest is Raymond Vernon, *Sovereignty at Bay* (New York: Basic Books, 1971).

17. S. Hymer and R. Rowthorn, 'Multinational corporations and international oligopoly: The non-American challenge', Yale Growth Center Discussion Paper No. 75, Sept. 1969, pp. 28–9.

18. Not all poor countries have responded passively, however. Some have been able to generate their own technology or adapt imported technology to local needs, and where this has been done on a massive scale the poor countries have been able to escape from the processes described in this chapter. Historically, Japan, and currently, Taiwan and possibly China, have managed to avoid adopting a passive or defensive position and have actively encouraged research and innovative activity.

19. W. Beckerman and R. Bacon, 'The international distribution of incomes', in P. P. Streeten (ed.), *Unfashionable Economics* (London: Weidenfeld and Nicolson, 1970) p. 62.

20. Ibid., p. 56.

21. It is well known that many poor countries not only are dependent on foreign trade in general, as we have seen, but also they are dependent on a very few products for export. For example, coffee accounts for 61 per cent of Colombia's exports, petroleum accounts for 89 per cent of Iran's exports, tea accounts for 56 per cent of Sri Lanka's exports, rice accounts for 50 per cent of Burma's exports, and cotton accounts for 78 per cent of Chad's exports.

22. This approach is carefully developed in W. M. Corden, 'The effects of trade on the rate of growth', in J. Bhagwati *et al.* (eds.), *Trade, Balance of Payments and Growth* (Amsterdam: North-Holland, 1971).

23. For a further development of this argument and application to a specific context see Keith Griffin, *Underdevelopment in Spanish America* (London: Allen and Unwin, 1969).

24. T. Balogh in collaboration with P. Balacs, 'Fact and fancy in international economic relations', *World Development* (Feb. 1973) p. 80. See also G. Haberler, 'Some problems in the pure theory of international trade', *Economic Journal* (June 1950).

25. T. Balogh, op. cit.

26. Sir John Hicks argues that 'the fact that force has been used in the establishment of a trading colony does not imply that the colony, after its establishment, is an exception to the principle of all-round advantage'. He then adds that to the indigenous people 'trade offers new opportunities, and these must represent in some sense a gain. They do indeed have to learn to make use of their opportunities; in the process of learning they will make mistakes, mistakes that will be costly, often very costly. But we can recognize the mistakes, and their consequences, without denying that the main trend must be advantageous'. *A Theory of Economic History* (London: Oxford University Press, 1969) pp. 51–2.

27. Ibid., p. 165.

28. The theoretical literature is beginning to take this phenomenon into account. See, for instance, M. Posner, 'International trade and technical change', *Oxford Economic Papers* (Oct. 1961); R. Vernon, 'International investment and international trade in the product cycle', *Quarterly Journal of Economics* (May 1966); G. D. Hufbauer, *Synthetic Materials and the Theory of International Trade* (London: Duckworth, 1966); M. Posner,

'Technical change, international trade and foreign investment', in P. P. Streeten (ed.), *Unfashionable Economics* (London: Weidenfeld and Nicolson, 1970). Also see the excellent paper by Frances Stewart, 'Trade and technology', in P. P. Streeten (ed.), *Trade Strategies for Development* (London: Macmillan, 1973).
29. R. W. Klein, 'A dynamic theory of comparative advantage', *American Economic Review* (Mar. 1973).
30. OECD, *Gaps in Technology. Analytical Report* (Paris, 1970).
31. W. Gruber, D. Mehta and R. Vernon, 'The R and D factor in international trade and international investment of US industries', *Journal of Political Economy* (Feb. 1967) Table 2, p. 24.
32. Comparative advantage is, of course, modified by tariffs, quotas, cartels, etc.
33. Note that this theory does *not* predict a continuous decline in the commodity terms of trade of underdeveloped countries. Indeed it could be consistent with an improvement in the commodity terms of trade, e.g. if marginal costs of exportables in the rich countries were falling faster than the price of exportables. Furthermore, our theory even permits an improvement in the single factoral terms of trade of underdeveloped countries. It predicts, however, that their double factoral terms of trade will decline, i.e. that the distribution of the gains from trade will tend to move in favour of rich countries. Note, too, that our analysis of unequal exchange has nothing in common with that of A. Emmanuel, *Unequal Exchange: A Study of the Imperialism of Trade* (New York: Monthly Review Press, 1972).
34. Sanjaya Lall, 'Transfer-pricing by multinational manufacturing firms', *Oxford Bulletin of Economics and Statistics* (Aug. 1973).
35. The cumulative disequilibrium is, of course, strengthened by the barriers imposed by the rich countries to the immigration of unskilled labour. See Ch. 4.
36. Information Division of the Treasury, *Economic Progress Report*, No. 40 (June 1973).
37. It could be argued that one explanation for the lower return on investment in underdeveloped countries is specific supply bottlenecks and a lack of complementary factors of production. For instance, acute shortages of power or transport in construction materials might reduce the rate of return in all industries other than in the bottleneck industries or sector. Moreover, especially if the bottleneck is a non-traded good and the gestation period of investment is lengthy, supply shortages may persist for a considerable time, thereby depressing profit rates and the expectations of businessmen.
38. John Dunning has estimated that the marginal rate of return on UK direct investment, in the period 1960–5, was 7.1 per cent in the underdeveloped countries and 12.6 per cent in the developed countries. His data do not include investments in oil, banking and insurance. See J. H. Dunning, *Studies in International Investment* (London: Allen and Unwin, 1970) pp. 57, 66.
39. For example, by the end of 1966 the notorious Investors Overseas Services had an investment fund of more than $500 million and at least 40 per cent of these resources came from underdeveloped countries. See Charles Raw,

Bruce Page and Godfrey Hodgson, *Do You Sincerely Want to be Rich?* (Harmondsworth: Penguin, 1972).

40. The outflow of savings from the underdeveloped countries will tend to undermine their balance of payments position. They may react in a variety of ways: by running down the reserves, by reducing aggregate demand, by seeking foreign aid and borrowing abroad, by giving additional incentives to direct investment by foreigners, by imposing controls on outward capital movements, by encouraging exports and discouraging imports through devaluation, tariffs, subsidies, etc.

41. Arnold Harberger has estimated that the return on all capital employed in Colombia (public and private, manufacturing and non-manufacturing sectors) was between 8.3 and 10.4 per cent, depending on the assumptions made. See his *Project Evaluation* (London: Macmillan, 1970) Ch. 6, Tables 6.18 and 6.20.

42. Some underdeveloped countries may, of course, from time to time encounter windfall gains, such as the discovery of oil or of other valuable natural resources or the opening up of new markets because of tariff preferences, etc. These windfall gains may permit rapid growth for a period, but they are unlikely to be sustained and hence are unlikely to enable a country to escape from the processes perpetuating underdevelopment.

2. Multinational corporations and basic needs development

One of the most striking features of the international economy in the last quarter-century is the growth of the multinational corporation as the propelling force of world trade and production. The multinationals are not a new phenomenon, of course. Indeed, they were an important instrument of European penetration into Asia, Africa and the Americas during the 17th century and the early colonial period. In recent decades, however, the range of their operations has increased enormously, spreading rapidly from mineral and oil extraction and the production and marketing of plantation crops, where they were long dominant, to manufacturing and a broad range of service activities. Moreover, the scale of their operations, their control of technological and marketing information and their ability to operate in several countries have given these corporations a peculiar strength in international relations. This strength rarely is matched by an equivalent countervailing governmental power in most of the underdeveloped countries in which they operate.

The power of the multinational corporations could in principle be either a malevolent or a benevolent influence, depending on the particular economic and political context in which they operate. At one extreme they can be viewed as an instrument for improving the world-wide allocation of resources, as a means of expanding international commerce, as an engine of national economic growth and as an instrument for supplying the basic needs of the poor.[1] Thus, according to this view, multinational enterprises essentially are enterprises that serve the world. They are usually subject to competitive pressures or else can be controlled by government policy.[2] Thus the multinationals are little more than enlarged versions of the corner grocery store or city builder and like them are concerned with satisfying the basic needs of the population. At its extreme this vision becomes so idyllic that it is difficult

42

to distinguish between the Ford Motor Company and the Ford Foundation. Associated with this view of the multinationals is the belief that the interests of the companies and of the countries are so compatible that they can be reconciled merely by calling for 'good citizenship' on the part of each.[3]

At the other extreme, multinational corporations can be viewed as vehicles for monopolistic exploitation which perpetuate the subordination of poor countries by the rich, as devices which tend systematically to channel the economic surplus of poor countries into non-essential activities and consequently as obstacles to basic needs development. According to this view, the multinationals are the devil incorporated, if not incarnate.

I. MULTINATIONALS AS BLACK BOXES

At the simplest level the multinational corporation can be regarded as an invisible black box which merely combines labour and material inputs and transforms them into intermediate and final products. In the process of doing so, value added is generated and this results in higher incomes for those who supply labour and the means of production and for governments which tax these incomes. The black box can do no harm, only good.

The worst that can happen, in a limiting case, is that a country would receive zero benefit from the operation of multinational corporations. This would arise if all labour and material inputs were imported, all production exported, all the equity and loan capital were supplied by foreigners and all net profits repatriated, and none of the profits were taxed by the government of the host country. In this case, no additional direct employment would be created, no income-earning opportunities would arise for local people to supply goods, services or finance capital, and no revenue would be received by the government. The multinational corporation would be irrelevant but not harmful. Under less extreme circumstances there is a presumption that at least some groups in the host country would benefit, although the distribution of the benefits between the foreign company and the host population might be highly unequal, and thus the world distribution of income might become less equitable.

The qualified optimism of these conclusions rests on the assumption that the sales and purchases of the foreign corporation in the domestic market are at competitive prices. If a multinational corporation is able to establish a monopoly position in the host economy it may inflict losses on local consumers by forcing them to pay higher prices than necessary. Similarly, if it is able to acquire a monopsony position it may inflict losses on its workers and suppliers.

Both phenomena have been important historically. Multinational corporations were traditionally active in public utilities where the 'natural monopoly' element of such activities as electricity and urban transport gave them access to high, monopolistic profits. Given that many public utilities are a central component of any basic needs strategy for development, monopolistic exploitation in this sector is almost certain to be felt disproportionately by the poor. Increasingly, however, governments have taken over these natural monopolies and multinationals have almost disappeared from these activities.

The monopsonistic organisation of the labour force has been common, particularly in the mineral economies of southern and central Africa[4] and in the plantation economies of Central America and the Caribbean islands.[5] The exercise of this form of power has by no means been eradicated, but the combination of progressive labour legislation, nationalisation[6] and greater competition is rapidly reducing its incidence.

The general point remains valid, however. The growth of multinationals is inherently oligopolistic, and in its contemporary form is based on advanced technology and sophisticated marketing techniques supplemented by the economies of large-scale production. It should become clear in the course of this chapter that this type of oligopolistic growth, its extension internationally, and the fundamental forces that both facilitate and accompany it, are incompatible with basic needs development regardless of particular policy measures adopted by government.

Of course, a different and specific set of problems does arise from the policies of the governments of host countries. A multinational corporation's activities may be harmful to a country in social terms if it is given privileges and inappropriate incentives. Thus high protection for agricultural and manufacturing undertakings (including exemption of tariffs on capital equipment, tax holidays, the provision of low-cost finance capital—sometimes at negative real rates of interest—and excessive export incentives) enable large multinational corporations and the national groups allied to them to make monopolistic profits. In some cases the value added to the economy will be negative at international prices, so that production actually reduces the real income of the economy, despite the fact that it may be highly profitable to the corporation. In such cases there will also be a balance of payments cost because there will be a net outflow of capital which will not be compensated by improved overall efficiency and output for the economy.

Some writers have emphasised the role of multinationals in stimulating local entrepreneurship, particularly through subcontracting arrangements with small national suppliers.[7] Others have argued, however, that the net effect of the activities of foreign corporations is more likely to be a reduction in local entrepreneurship than an increase.[8] Whatever may be the 'pure' effect of multinationals on the supply of entrepreneurship, local initiative and innovation are likely to be discouraged by the types of policies one typically encounters in countries relying on multinational enterprises for development.

Government policies often discriminate against small firms through complex licensing arrangements, by imposing artificial ceilings on interest rates which result in credit being rationed in such a way that it is available only to large firms, and by discrimination in government procurement. These measures go directly counter to a basic needs development strategy and create an economic environment in which large firms, multinational as well as national, are sheltered from competition and given incentives to use excessively capital-intensive methods of production.

In some countries the systems of control over investment and production are so complex that only a large multinational corporation can afford the costs of going into business. It relies on subsequent monopolistic profits to recover its initial outlay. Yet local firms are often better equipped for production to serve small markets and for supplying the wage goods and other essential items required by the poor. Furthermore, an environment which encourages small firms to flourish is certain to be a more competitive one and is likely to encourage an active search for more appropriate technologies. A small firm, in addition, is usually less inclined toward vertical integration, so that it is more likely than a large corporation to rely on small, relatively labour-intensive local producers as suppliers.

Perhaps many would agree that in theory an economic system comprised of small, competitive firms would be more equitable and efficient, and hence more desirable, than a system dominated by oligopolies. The question that arises is whether, in a world of 'monopoly capitalism', it is politically possible to introduce a system of 'competitive capitalism'. If the answer to this query is 'no', then the social costs arising from monopolistic competition should be attributed not to the multinationals or to the government's policies but to the present form of capitalism.

Be this as it may, other socially harmful effects arise not from the consequences of specific government measures but from an inherent clash between national objectives and the international perspective of foreign corporations. Thus in evaluating the role of multinationals one must take into account not only the nature of industrial organisation (monopolistic or competitive) but also the structure of ownership (foreign or local). Three examples can be given. First, most countries, regardless of their form of social organisation and level of economic development, regard the local ownership of their productive resources as a matter of public interest. The ownership of natural resources—land and minerals—is usually regarded as being particularly important. Foreign ownership is thus a cost in itself. That is, capitalism may be tolerable in many countries, but a system in which the foreigners are the capitalists and the natives are the workers increasingly is not.

Of course the intrusion of foreign corporations into a society will have much more complex effects on the class composition of that society than the preceding sentence suggests. In many instances, particularly where multinationals provide wages and working conditions superior to the average,[9] they have contributed to a process of class differentiation through the creation of a local élite of intermediaries and workers. This 'labour aristocracy' sometimes identifies itself with foreign corporations, acquires vested interests in the perpetuation of a system in which the multinationals flourish, and often opposes changes of benefit to the majority of workers and the poor in general. This tendency to undermine national cohesion is a second example of how national and corporate interests can conflict.

Third, the multinational nature of a corporation may lead to conflicts and costs. Conflicts of interest between a country and a corporation may arise over the desirable rate of depletion of non-renewable resources, levels of production and export, and sources of supply of materials and services. Such conflicts will be exacerbated when the government of the home country attempts to exercise its sovereignty and imposes its political preferences on multinational corporations. The ability of the multinational corporations to evade monetary and fiscal regulations, because of the international character of their operations, is another source of friction and social cost. Also common is the manipulation of transfer prices between the branches of a multinational corporation to minimise taxation, evade exchange controls, avoid political friction and disputes with labour unions.[10]

II. THE INTERACTION OF MULTINATIONALS WITH THE ENVIRONMENT

The view of the multinational corporation as a black box is based on the implicit assumption that multinational corporations are profit-maximising institutions which, like the corner grocery store, accept the world as they find it and do the best they can. In fact, however, the multinationals do not respond passively, but actively attempt to influence the environment in which they operate. For example, they both satisfy existing demand and through their sales-promotion activities attempt to create new preferences, tastes and wants. (That such sales promotion is not peculiar or specific to multinational firms is clear, but this does not affect our argument.) In some instances the products of the multinationals merely replace locally-produced goods, sometimes of identical quality, but lacking an international brand in appealing to consumers. The production method may be less labour-intensive, although this is not always the case and, even when it is, this is sometimes offset by an improvement in quality or reduction in raw material use which represents a real cost reduction. In a highly protected economy, however, this is not necessarily passed on to consumers.

Cases have been found in which the foreign product is inferior to the local one. The most dramatic example is that of baby foods which are produced and sold by Nestlé and other multinationals as a substitute for breast feeding, a costless gift of Nature.

Most infant milk formula is sold in the Third World in powdered form and the powdered milk must be mixed with water before it is usable. As a result, in areas where the water is unclean or where fuel for sterilising bottles is scarce, it may be impossible to prepare the infant formula correctly. Consequently babies are fed contaminated food. The problem is compounded when poverty induces the mother to dilute the formula with more than the recommended amount of water. In these circumstances the use of powdered milk has led to malnutrition, to illnesses such as diarrhoea and to greater infant mortality.

The sales promotion techniques used by the multinationals, including sending 'mothercraft workers' dressed in nurses' uniforms to hospitals, clinics and individual homes to instruct new mothers on the advantages of the company formula, have contributed directly to increasing the health risk of newly-born babies. These practices, and their consequences, were first exposed by War on Want and later were condemned by the World Health Organization. As a result of the unfavourable publicity and the pressure of international public opinion, the baby-food manufacturers formed an International Council of the Infant Food Industries and in late 1975 announced an advertising code designed to reduce misleading and dangerous selling methods. Dangerous practices, alas, are not confined to food manufacturers. The multinationals of the pharmaceutical industry have an even more execrable record in the Third World. Indeed the unethical marketing practices of the corporations were vigorously denounced by the Director-General of WHO at the Organisation's World Health Assembly in 1975. The companies export and market in the Third World drugs which are not authorised for sale in the country of origin.[11] They sell drugs in the Third World at substantially higher prices than the identical drugs cost the consumer in the developed countries. They promote drugs as being effective in curing illnesses which are not so certified by the regulatory agencies in the country of origin. They sell products of substandard quality. They sell drugs beyond their date of expiry. Moreover, increasingly the Third World is being used as a testing ground for new drugs as a way of avoiding the stringent regulations on experimenting with human beings found in the United States and other developed countries. Finally, the multinational drug companies encourage the poor nations to waste scarce resources in purchasing medicaments which, if not actually harmful, are at best only marginally useful and often totally irrelevent to real health needs.[12]

The provision of adequate nutrition and health are essential ingredients of any basic needs strategy. The evidence so far available suggests that even in the few cases when the multinational corporations produce and market the type of goods which in principle could be consistent with such a strategy, they manage to pervert it. In many other cases, of course, the multinationals produce goods which are inconsistent with basic needs development. The reasons for this have less to do with the moral turpitude of the corporations than with the very nature of multinationals.

In a survey of the role of private industry in alleviating the nutrition problem Alan Berg has concluded that despite the substantial time and energy devoted by governments to involving big business, 'there is little to show in the way of nutrition improvement. Nor are the prospects bright for reaching a significant portion of the needy with proprietary foods marketed in the conventional manner'. Among the many problems, he indicates that 'the major impediment is the inability to reconcile the demand for corporate profit with a product low enough in cost to reach the needy in large numbers.'[13]

Investment by multinationals is often concentrated on consumer products developed for the mass markets of rich countries and which only middle and upper income groups in poor countries can afford.

Non-durable goods such as highly finished textiles produced from synthetic materials and durables such as washing machines and private motor cars are manufactured instead of low-cost textiles using locally-grown fibres, or laundry equipment, bicycles, trucks or buses. The sophisticated products often require relatively capital-intensive techniques of production and have limited possibilities of substituting men for machines. In this way the composition of output both reflects and reinforces initial inequalities in the distribution of income.

The general point is that the adoption of a basic needs strategy of development will require a reallocation of resources toward the production of commodities demanded by low income groups (semi-processed foodstuffs, coarse clothing, inexpensive crockery) and the capital goods required to produce them (including hand tools and simple power-driven equipment). It is unlikely that multinational corporations, accustomed to producing internationally standardised products in large volume with highly mechanised techniques, will have a competitive advantage in supplying these goods.

Capital-intensive production on a small scale is usually inefficient and therefore costly. As a result, the prices of such goods are generally above international prices, thereby limiting further the expansion of the market and of employment. The component inputs tend to be sophisticated, requiring complex and diversified supplying industries. This tends to delay the possibility of producing components and material inputs efficiently, and to necessitate the presence of multinationals in the industries with backward linkages. Thus undesirable effects are likely to reinforce each other, while the opposite will be true of desirable effects. For example, the type of steel plant a country requires will be affected by the sophistication of the products for which it is a supplier. A choice of products appropriate to the mass of consumers will tend to lead to the choice of employment-intensive techniques of production. This, in turn, will generate employment multiplier effects and hence a more rapidly expanding market for such products with further employment effects. Thus any undue influence by the multinationals in favour of an inappropriate choice of products is likely to have widespread consequences throughout the economy.

Once the distribution of income and the sales activities of the multinationals and local firms have determined the composition of output, however, there appears to be little difference between the multinational corporations and large indigenous enterprises in the choice of technique or degree of capacity utilisation. That is, given the environment, including relative factor prices and the general policy context, large firms, whether locally or foreign owned, behave in much the same way as regards the degree of capital intensity. In this respect only, the multinational corporations and large local firms are similar.

It would be wrong to imagine, however, that multinational corporations merely respond passively to the policy context in which they happen to be located. On the contrary, there is a complex interaction or mutual causation between government policies and the behaviour of large international corporations. Government measures evidently affect the behaviour of the firm: they influence whether the firm will produce or not, what type of technology will be used, the nature of the product that will be sold and the market that will be available, the conditions under which labour will be employed, the volume of profit after tax and the amount that can be repatriated.

Equally, the multinational corporations attempt to influence, often with success, the policies governments choose to implement. This influence is not confined to the details of fiscal, monetary or licensing regulations but extends, as recent international scandals testify, to intervention into the national political processes of host countries. One multinational corporation (ITT) has recently been exposed for attempting to enlist a foreign intelligence agency (the CIA) in overthrowing the government of a then socialist country (Chile); the president of another (United Brands) was found to have bribed a Head of State (Honduras) and to have secured a reduction in an export tax and successfully destroyed a banana exporters' cartel; while another multinational corporation operating in a southern European nation (Italy) donated huge sums of money to several political parties in an apparently successful attempt to safeguard its interests.[14]

Exactly how much money has been spent by multinational corporations in an attempt to mould the world to their wishes is of course unknown. An incomplete list of 'improper payments overseas made by American corporations', culled from various US newspapers and published in *The Economist*,[15] indicates that Exxon leads the league with $46 to 49 million. Among the drug companies, Merck and Co. are alleged to have distributed $3.6 million and Upjohn $2.7 million; among the food industries, United Brands appears to have spent $2 million and Carnation $1.2 million.

The efforts of the multinationals are not limited to subversion, bribery and unscrupulous attempts to purchase good will: not all faces of capitalism are so blatantly 'unacceptable' (to use Mr Heath's phrase).

Nor do the corporations limit themselves to dealing directly with governments; indirect methods too are employed, including attempts to influence the policy of international agencies. For example, the interests of big business are formally entrenched in the tripartite structure of the International Labour Organisation, and have been so since its establishment in 1919. More recently, the multinationals have infiltrated the United Nations Food and Agriculture Organization, particularly through its Industry Cooperative Programme and its Bankers' Programme.[16] The latter is a growing club of 30 national development banks and about 15 major commercial banks, including American Express, Barclays International and the First National City Bank.

These anecdotes, scraps of evidence and dramatic episodes illustrate a mundane point, namely, that the multinationals do not take policies as 'given', but energetically attempt to influence the economic, social and political environment in which they pursue their quest for profit. If a government allows these corporations to become established within its frontiers it must be prepared to accept them on these terms.

III. A FOREIGN PACKAGE

Having accepted them, a country is likely to find that the multinationals provide not a single, specific service but a complex of services which are difficult to untangle. Perhaps most obvious is the role of the multinational corporation in international capital flows. But the transfer of capital is not the only, or even the principal, transfer made by foreign corporations. Indeed, as much as three-quarters of the overseas investment undertaken by multinational corporations is financed either by retained earnings of the local subsidiary or from local savings mobilised in the capital market.[17] The multinational provides a 'package' of capital, technology, marketing and management skill, or a mixture of those components in varying proportions. The strength of the multinational is not confined to the production process, but stretches from the purchasing of raw materials, through production, to transport and marketing.

The strength of the multinational, however, is not synonymous with benefit to the Third World. The difficulty is that the multinational may do too much rather than too little. All of the components of the 'package' have their cost to the host country and earn an income for the corporation, yet not all the desirable components may be missing in the host economy and some of the components may be undesirable or even harmful. For instance, the technology that is employed by the multi-national may be inappropriate to local resource endowments, and better technologies for the same product may be available locally, but international marketing outlets may be absent. A multinational corporation might be able to solve the marketing problem, but in so doing it might aggravate the employment problem and existing income inequalities by introducing unnecessarily capital-intensive methods of production.

Ideally, governments of host countries ought to specify which of the components of the package supplied by multinationals is not available locally and then examine whether it is possible to obtain the missing component more cheaply from another source. For example, if capital is the missing ingredient, it may be possible to obtain it more cheaply from foreign commercial banks; if management is lacking, it may be possible to negotiate a management contract for a fixed period; if technology is unavailable, a royalty agreement may be possible, etc. If governments can induce or compel the multinationals to untie their package, a more selective approach can be adopted and the net benefits to the host economy can thereby be increased.

This is easier said than done, however. A major reason for this is that the strength of the multinational corporation arises from the fact that it operates in a monopolistic market. Indeed, many of its investment decisions, sales techniques and research activities are designed to perpetuate market imperfections and if possible accentuate them. The presentation of its offerings in the form of a 'package' is simply another way in which the multinational attempts to safeguard its market position. If the 'package' is untied, the strength of the multinational will be reduced, and precisely for this reason any attempt to do so will be resisted.

IV. SEARCHING FOR BETTER BARGAINS

The possibility of untying the 'package', and the terms on which this can be done, will depend upon the outcome of a process of bargaining rather than on the consequences of unadulterated market forces. Thus the benefits an underdeveloped country can expect to receive depend in part on the power, determination, sophistication and information possessed by its negotiators. Evidently negotiating ability varies considerably from time to time, from country to country, and from industry to industry. The bargain is likely to be relatively less favourable in countries in which a significant section of the ruling class is closely allied to the interests of multinational corporations. It is likely to be more favourable in large countries, or in a situation in which several countries act in concert—as in the Andean Group—than in small countries acting in isolation. It is likely to be less favourable the more multinationals there are operating in a country, particularly if many of the corporations are from a single country.

Finally, the outcome of oligopolistic bargaining is likely to be more favourable the more knowledge the negotiators have at their disposal. The exposure in the press of the most glaring transgressions of the multinationals is important, as in the Nestlé case. The establishment of a United Nations Centre on Transnational Corporations is another small step toward formulating a framework in which the behaviour of the multinationals in the world economy can be scrutinised.

The accumulation of studies of particular aspects of international corporations, such as systems of transfer pricing used by vertically-integrated firms, is helpful. More generally, the exchange of information on the type and nature of existing contracts, ideally by an international body constituted for that purpose,[18] would strengthen the bargaining position of national negotiators. Lastly, governments anxious to maximise the benefits that can be extracted from large multinational enterprises should arm themselves with technical advice from specialists knowledgeable in the affairs of the industry. A politician or general civil servant, however able he may be, is at a serious disadvantage when confronted by the expertise that can be marshalled by the negotiators for the multinationals.

All this, of course, begs the decisive question: is it possible on balance, and apart from isolated instances, to reach a bargain with multinational corporations which is in the interests of the poor?

V. MULTINATIONALS AND A BASIC NEEDS STRATEGY

The answer would appear to be self-evidently in the affirmative to some observers. A great many underdeveloped countries, or at least the governments of underdeveloped countries, have 'revealed' their preferences by encouraging multinational corporations to produce and market their goods domestically.[19] Moreover, it has been argued, the corporations have changed in recent years, or have been forced to change. No longer do they insist on 100 per cent ownership of local subsidiaries; joint ventures with local capitalists or the government are common; even minority foreign holdings are becoming more acceptable to the multinationals. More local staff have been employed and the most progressive firms have recruited technicians and management personnel locally. The corporations, in short, have become more flexible and have demonstrated their ability to adapt to changing political and economic circumstances.

It remains to be seen, however, whether the multinational corporations have a role to play in basic needs development.

One point at least seems clear: the impact of the multinationals on total employment is likely to remain insignificant. Hence, in so far as the implementation of a basic needs strategy requires a large increase in employment, the multinationals have little to contribute.

Estimates of the stock of overseas assets held by multinational corporations are subject to substantial margins of error, but a reasonable figure is that, as of 1970, direct foreign investment amounted to $40.7 thousand million, of which half was located in Latin America and the Caribbean. This stock of foreign-owned assets provided employment for approximately 2 million persons in the Third World, or roughly 0.3 per cent of the active population.[20] The average cost of creating a job by the multinationals thus turns out to be in excess of $20,000. In other words, in comparison with the magnitude of the problem, the effects of the multinationals in generating employment are negligible.

Of course, a basic needs strategy would reduce the incentives which now exist to introduce relatively capital-intensive methods of production, and as a result, any given volume of investment would in future create more jobs. But the same strategy which reduced the bias in favour of mechanisation would also reduce several of the special advantages enjoyed by the multinationals. First, the domestic market for Western-designed, mass-produced consumer durables would contract. Second, opportunities for manipulating demand and creating new tastes through sophisticated marketing techniques would diminish. Third, the profitability of the technology used by the multinationals would fall. Hence, basic needs development would probably imply a reduced need on the part of the underdeveloped countries for the services which the multinational corporations can best supply.

In addition to a contraction in direct private foreign investment, the implementation of a basic needs strategy would probably result also in a change in its composition. The demand for wage goods would expand, as would the demand for intermediate and capital goods related to the provision of basic needs. Flexible firms, local and foreign, capable of producing efficient technologies corresponding to local resource endowments would encounter increased opportunities as well as more intense competition. A few multinationals already supply goods consumed largely by those with below-average incomes, e.g. sewing machines, and their activities could increase. Often, perhaps, this will be by greater use of local subcontractors, thereby encouraging local entrepreneurship.

Basic needs development, if adopted in many countries, should create more opportunities for underdeveloped countries to trade with and invest in each other. New types of multinationals might emerge— smaller, more competitive firms based in poor countries—as is happening in Latin America today. These firms would supply different types of commodities produced with different types of technologies. Their activities would tend to reinforce a more equal distribution of income rather than undermine it as at present. Even in this ideal situation the role of multinational corporations would remain essentially marginal to wider development processes, but the pattern envisaged here implies that they could become marginally favourable rather than the reverse. In any situation short of the neoclassical ideal, however, multinationals are more likely to constitute part of the problem than part of the solution.

NOTES AND REFERENCES

1. For a definition of basic needs and a discussion of basic needs development, see ILO, *Employment, Growth and Basic Needs* (Geneva, 1976).
2. 'The most important determinant of the multinationals' role in a particular developing country is the development strategy adopted by the government and people of the country in question.' Ibid., p. 166.
3. Ibid., p. 169. The optimism of the conventional reasoning reflected in the ILO document follows from the assumption of neo-classical welfare economics, its definition of welfare, its assumption of competition and its ideology of social harmony. For an extended discussion of this see Sanjaya Lall and Paul Streeten, *Foreign Investment, Transnationals and Developing Countries* (London: Macmillan, 1977, Ch. 3).
4. For a recent study of a formal colonial situation see Charles van Onselen, *Chibaro: African Mine Labour in Southern Rhodesia, 1900–1933* (London: Pluto Press, 1976).
5. See, for example, George L. Beckford, 'The Economics of Agriculture Resource Use and Development in Plantation Economies', *Social and Economic Studies* (Dec. 1969).
6. Between 1956 and 1972, foreign enterprises equivalent to about 25 per cent of the total foreign-owned capital stock in the underdeveloped countries in 1972 were nationalised. The incidence of nationalisation was especially high in mining and smelting, agriculture and public utilities. See M. L. Williams,

'The Extent and Significance of the Nationalization of Foreign-owned Assets in Developing Countries, 1956–1972', *Oxford Economic Papers* (July 1975).

7. See, for example, Susumu Watanabe, 'Entrepreneurship in Small Enterprises in Japanese Manufacturing', *International Labour Review* (Dec. 1970); see also by the same author 'International Subcontracting, Employment and Skill Promotion', *International Labour Review* (May 1972); and 'Subcontracting, Industrialization and Employment Creation', *International Labour Review* (July-Aug. 1971).

8. A. O. Hirschman, *How to Divest in Latin America, and Why* (Princeton: Essays in International Finance, 76, Nov. 1969).

9. Wages paid by multinationals in the manufacturing and mineral sectors, in contrast to plantations, are often nowadays above the national average. For some evidence see ILO, *Wages and Working Conditions in International Enterprises* (Geneva, 1976).

10. See, for example, C. V. Vaitsos, *Intercountry Income Distribution and Transnational Corporations* (Oxford: Clarendon Press, 1974); Sanjaya Lall, 'Transfer Pricing by Multinational Manufacturing Firms'. *Oxford Bulletin of Economics and Statistics* (Aug. 1973).

11. Apparently 'in Mexico there are now four times as many drugs on sale as in the U.S.' See Ivan Illich, *Medical Nemesis* (London: Calder and Boyars, 1975), p. 41.

12. See 'Drug Companies and the Third World', *New Scientist* (29 Apr. 1976); for a detailed study, see Sanjaya Lall, 'Major Issues in Transfer of Technology to Developing Countries: A Case Study of the Pharmaceutical Industry' (UNCTAD TD/B/C.6/4, 8 Oct 1975).

13. Alan Berg, *The Nutrition Factor* (Washington: Brookings Institution, 1973), p. 158.

14. In addition to the multinationals engaging in direct investment, the role of large corporations engaged in systematic export promotion (such as Lockheed) needs to be considered.

15. *The Economist* (3 Apr. 1976), p. 41.

16. See the article by Erich H. Jacoby, a retired FAO official, in *Le Monde Diplomatique* (4 July 1976), pp. 4–5. In Jacoby's opinion: 'A l'heure actuelle, dans bon nombre de pays sous-développés, il existe de toute évidence un lien de cause à effet entre l'implantation des sociétés transnationales et le danger imminent de famine.'

17. The contribution of private foreign capital to investment is much exaggerated, whereas its significance for the control of the economy is much neglected.

18. See Paul Streeten, 'Policies towards Multinationals', *World Development* (June 1975).

19. This in itself proves nothing, however, unless one believes in the social neutrality of the state and denies that governments are the embodiment of a balance of class forces.

20. United Nations, *Multinational Corporations in World Development* (1973).

3. Foreign capital, domestic savings and economic development

I. INTRODUCTION

The flow of official aid from the members of the OECD Development Assistance Committee rose rapidly until 1961. Thenceforward, however, the total increased rather slowly. In 1961 net official aid, i.e. gross disbursements minus amortisation, was $5,210 million; in 1968 it was $6,471 million. [1] This represents an increase over the period of less than a quarter and a trend rate of growth of about 3.1 per cent a year. In the period 1962–8 the annual average rate of increase was 2.5 per cent, i.e. exactly equal to the rate of increase of the population in the underdeveloped countries. In other words, the amount of foreign aid available *per caput* has not increased since 1962.

Most of the aid disbursed is bilateral; most of the aid is tied to purchases from donor countries; and an increasing proportion of the aid is in the form of loans. Bilateral grants in 1968 were $3,377 million, the smallest sum in the current decade. In fact, grants accounted for over three-quarters of all aid in 1960 but now represent little more than half. As a consequence of these factors and the continued world-wide inflation, real aid *per caput* undoubtedly is falling in the underdeveloped countries. [2]

These tendencies are disturbing to many economists, yet the situation that confronts the underdeveloped countries is much worse than the above figures imply. In fact, many poor regions of the world are net contributors of resources to the rich nations. In Latin America, for instance, it has been calculated that in the period 1950–61 the region was a net contributor of resources to the United States of about $174 million a year. [3] Despite the efforts exerted under the Alliance for Progress programme the position has changed only slightly since then, as Table 7 demonstrates.

TABLE 7.   Capital movements in Latin America, annual average
1961–1968 (million of dollars)

1.	AID grants[a]	131.4
2.	Foreign loans[b]	938.0
3.	Amortisation of foreign loans	-310.9
4.	Interest on foreign loans	-186.8
5.	Net movement of foreign grants and loans	571.7
6.	US direct private investment	360.5
7.	Profit and interest repayments on (6)[c]	-1063.1
8.	Net movement of private capital[c]	-702.6
9.	Net movement of all capital	-130.9

Source: Organisation of American States.

[a] Figures for grants refer to authorisations, not disbursements.
[b] Loans of the World Bank Group, AID, Export-Import Bank
and the Inter-American Development Bank.
[c] Average of the period 1960–7.

In the period under consideration there was an average yearly inflow
of public grants and loans, after deducting amortisation and interest
charges, of approximately $572 million. This was more than offset,
however, by a net outflow of resources related to private foreign capital
of about $703 million. The net contribution of all foreign capital
movements (when repayment obligations are taken into account) was to
aggravate Latin America's balance of payments difficulties by $131
million a year. Assuming such a programme is politically feasible, these
figures imply that if Latin America were to forego all foreign aid,
renounce the foreign debt and confiscate all foreign investments, the
region would probably gain well over a thousand million dollars a
decade. Of course, such a strategy of 'self-help' would not be welcomed
or perhaps even tolerated by the donor nations, but—as I shall try to
demonstrate below—it would probably contribute more to the economic development of the region than any conceivable aid programme.
In fact, it is possible that capital imports, rather than accelerating
development, have in some cases retarded it.

II.   THE ORTHODOX MACRO-ECONOMICS OF AID

Many models have been constructed which attempt to show how capital
imports alter the aggregate performance of an economy.[4] The great
majority of these models are 'Keynesian' in spirit and rely on fixed
'technical' relationships (e.g. the incremental output-capital ratio) and

stable savings and import propensities. These models assume, almost without exception, first, that the rate of development will increase if the ratio of investment to national income rises and, secondly, that the investment ratio will rise if capital imports increase. Neither of these assumptions is wholly correct.

It is now generally agreed, I believe, that increased investment is neither necessary nor sufficient to achieve a high rate of growth in an underdeveloped country. In some circumstances expenditure on investment goods may have a negative return and expenditure on certain items usually classified as consumption may have a high positive return. It is less widely accepted that capital imports often tend to increase aggregate consumption more than investment. The reason this last point has not been accepted is that the possibility of capital imports supplementing consumption has been excluded from the typical aid model.

(a) *The savings gap*
The usual point of departure is the Harrod growth equation: $g = sk$, where g is the proportional rate of growth of national income, s is the proportion of national income saved and invested, and k is the incremental output – capital ratio. If a country receives a grant of aid a, expressed as a fraction of its national income, the growth rate rises to $g = (s + a)k$.

If g^* is a target or planned rate of growth and if k is assumed to be constant, one can deduce the rate of capital accumulation c necessary to achieve the target: $g^*/k = c$. The difference between c and s indicates the savings gap or the amount of aid necessary to achieve the target: $(c - s) = a$.

Some economists argue that the marginal propensity to save is higher than the average, i.e. $s' > s$, so that a given inflow of foreign aid has two effects: first, it supplements domestic savings and leads to a higher rate of accumulation of capital; and secondly, it raises income *per caput* and hence the proportion of income saved.[5] As a result, foreign aid increases a country's capacity for growth. Eventually, it is argued, the target rate of growth will become 'self-sustaining', i.e. the need for further assistance will cease.

It should be noted, however, that even if all the assumptions of the model are valid, 'self-sustained' growth would be achieved only if $s' > g^*/k$.[6] The larger the savings gap, i.e. the greater $(c - s)$, the less likely is the above condition to be satisfied, since the larger the 'gap' the more must the marginal propensity to save exceed the average in order eventually to close it.

(b) *The foreign exchange gap*

Some economists believe that the difficulties experienced by many underdeveloped countries arise not from their inability or unwillingness to save but from their inability to acquire foreign exchange by exporting. Accordingly, these economists view the role of aid not as supplementing savings but as supplementing foreign exchange earnings.

In aid and trade models the volume and value of exports is given or autonomous, so that one can write $X = \overline{X}$. The requirements for imports M, on the other hand, are rigidly determined by the level of income Y and the propensity to import: $M = mY$. Given the desired level or rate of growth of national income, the demand for foreign exchange to finance imports may exceed the supply of foreign exchange obtained from exports. If this happens, a 'foreign exchange gap' may arise which would reduce the rate of growth unless it is filled by foreign aid. The absolute size of the gap is equal to $(mY - \overline{X})$. This can be expressed in proportional terms and rewritten as $a = m - \overline{X}/Y$ to make it comparable to the notation used in the previous section.

The implication of models which stress the 'foreign exchange gap' is that potential domestic savings are being frustrated because at least some of the capital goods necessary to undertake desired investment are not produced domestically and cannot be obtained from abroad. If additional foreign exchange were available, the level of investment and the rate of growth would increase. Indeed, unless the import content of investment were 100 per cent, an increase in foreign assistance of £A should lead to a rise in capital formation of some multiple of A. To be precise, the increase in investment should equal £A/n, where n is the import content of investment expressed as a ratio. In other words, under these circumstances greater aid would not only raise the level of investment but it would also permit an increase in domestic savings.[7]

(c) *The binding constraint*

The two major gaps which foreign capital might fill have been briefly considered. In an *ex post* or accounting sense, however, these two gaps must be equal, since national income must be exactly equal to national expenditure. This accounting rule is clearly expressed by the identity $I + X \equiv S + M$. The terms can be rearranged and written in our previous notation as

$$a = c - s \equiv m - \overline{X}/Y$$

Ex ante, however, there is no reason why the savings gap should be identical to the foreign exchange gap, and many economists argue that donors should provide sufficient aid to fill whichever of the two gaps is the larger.

The weakness of this argument is that it assumes that domestic and foreign resources cannot be substituted. Suppose, *ex ante*, that $(m - \bar{X}/Y) > (c - s)$ and foreign exchange is therefore the binding constraint. In this case the theory implies that although domestic production can be increased—and the community is willing to refrain from consuming too much of it—it is impossible either to increase exports or to substitute domestic production for imports. Output which is not consumed can neither be sold abroad nor used to replace goods purchased abroad.

One can accept the proposition that most underdeveloped countries do not have flexible economies—and in fact I have argued thus myself[8]—but the degree of inflexibility assumed in the two-gap model surely is excessive. In the long run—and the analytic basis of these gaps is a long-run growth model—no economy is so rigid that it can neither produce capital goods, nor export goods nor import substitutes. It is possible, of course, that a government is unwilling rather than unable to introduce policies which would earn or save foreign exchange. In such a case it might appear that foreign exchange is the binding constraint, but it is the unwillingness to reduce domestic consumption in order to expand exports or reduce imports which is the source of the difficulty. In other words, ultimately there can only be one constraint on investment, viz. savings. This being so, the way is now clear to examine the relationship between foreign capital and domestic savings.

III. AID AND CONSUMPTION

The savings-gap model described above is based on the assumption that any increase in foreign capital is devoted entirely to raising the rate of capital accumulation. In other words, aid supplements domestic savings rather than consumption. The alternative view, which I shall attempt to defend, is that aid is essentially a substitute for savings and that a large fraction of foreign capital is used to increase consumption rather than investment.

If one takes planned growth rates seriously this is what one would expect to happen. That is, governments have, and are encouraged by aid agencies to have, growth targets. From these targets and an assumption about the incremental output – capital ratio, the amount of investment needed to achieve the target can be estimated. This investment can be financed either from domestic savings or from capital imports. Assuming the government wants to achieve its growth objective at the lowest possible cost in terms of reduced current consumption, it will substitute foreign capital for domestic savings to the fullest extent possible.

It might be claimed that in so far as foreign aid is tied to specific projects it would not be possible to switch aid from investment to consumption. This argument, however, is fallacious.

At one time it was believed that when an aid agency such as the World Bank financed a particular investment project, the resources channelled into that project really were financing that particular project and none other. Indeed the International Bank for Reconstruction and Development (IBRD) used to take pride in the 'soundness' and high economic return of some of its projects. It soon became recognised, however, that foreign capital was financing not the project to which it apparently was tied but the marginal investment project, i.e. of all those projects undertaken, the one that ranked lowest on a list of priorities.[9] Thus aid was financing not the most attractive but the least attractive, or marginal, project. This is what is meant, in fact, when it is said that aid is 'fungible'.

There is no reason to stop at this point, however. The 'fungibility' of aid is not restricted in any way. That is, foreign capital finances not the marginal investment project but the marginal expenditure project, and expenditure on the margin is just as likely (perhaps more likely) to be on consumption goods as on capital goods. Foreign capital represents a transfer of resources or purchasing power from one nation to another, and how these additional resources will be used cannot be determined *a priori*. There certainly is no presumption that none will be used to increase consumption.

This point can be demonstrated formally.

The choice made by a government or a community between present and future consumption (C_t and C_{t+1}, respectively) can be represented in terms of indifference curves and a budget line, as in Figure 4. The slope of the indifference curve reflects the government's or the community's time preference and the slope and position of the budget line are determined by the amount of resources available to be allocated and the rate of return on investment (which is assumed to be equal to the rate of interest). Initially equilibrium is at E.

Now assume that EG amount of foreign aid becomes available to the government. This shifts the budget line $b_1 b_1$ to the right, to $b_2 b_2$, as shown in the diagram. Under no circumstances would either present or

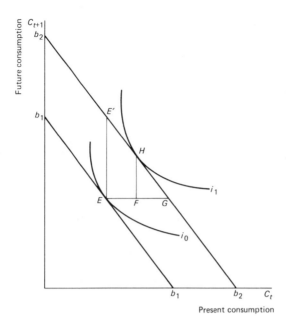

FIGURE 4

future consumption decline, since neither of these bundles of goods can be considered 'inferior'. In general, one would expect the resources provided through foreign aid to be allocated between consumption and investment in such a way that the opportunity cost of current consumption is exactly equal to the satisfaction obtained from consuming one additional item. It is conceivable, as is assumed in the savings-gap model, that the new equilibrium position would be directly above E, i.e. at E', so that C_t remained constant, but it is most unlikely. Normally, one would expect the new equilibrium to be some point such as H, at which both C_t and C_{t+1} are higher than originally.

In Figure 4 a capital inflow of EG leads to a rise in current consumption (or fall in domestic savings) of EF. Only FG amount of the aid supplements investment and this leads to an increase in future consumption of FH. In other words, a significant part of the foreign capital inflow is offset by a decline in domestic savings. In terms of the diagram, the proportion of foreign capital consumed is equal to EF/EG.

If the inflow of foreign aid were quite large relative to the total investment programme, the marginal productivity of capital and the real rate of interest might decline. A fall in the rate of interest, in turn, would tend to reduce domestic savings still further.[10] That is, the slope of the line $b_2 b_2$ would decline and a positive 'substitution effect' would reinforce the 'income effect', thereby further increasing the likelihood that foreign aid would supplement current consumption more than capital accumulation. I do not wish to stress this 'interest rate effect', however, because I shall argue below that a more important consequence of foreign aid is to alter the composition of investment in such a way that the marginal output – capital ratio k is lowered.

Having demonstrated that in theory one ought to expect a foreign capital inflow to reduce domestic savings, the next step is to consider whether this occurs in practice. As far as I know there has been no systematic study of this issue, but there is some empirical evidence that can be mentioned. Much of this evidence has emerged as a by-product of research on other topics; thus the results must be viewed as tentative. Much of the evidence is based on cross-section data and may not, therefore, tell us very much about the behaviour of an economy over time. Finally, the quality of much of the data is poor: domestic savings are calculated as a residual and the net inflow of foreign capital is assumed to be equal to the deficit on current account of the balance of payments. Despite these deficiencies, however, the results of regression analysis are highly suggestive.

A cross-section study of 32 underdeveloped countries, using United Nations data, gave the following results:

$$\frac{S}{Y} = 11.2 - 0.73\frac{A}{Y}; \ R^2 = 0.54$$
$$(0.11)$$

where S/Y = gross domestic savings as a per cent of GDP, 1962–4 and A/Y = foreign savings as a per cent of GDP, 1962–4.

Within the sample of 32 countries, 13 were from Asia and the Middle East. A similar regression for these countries produced similar results:

$$\frac{S}{Y} = 16.1 - 0.82\frac{A}{Y}; \ R^2 = 0.71$$
$$(0.52)$$

A group from the Organisation of American States recently calculated a savings function for 18 Latin American countries using data from *c.* 1960. Their findings are consistent with those cited above:[11]

$$S_t = 0.1716Y_t - 0.6702A_t; \ R^2 = 0.75$$
$$(0.005) \qquad (0.204)$$

Thus the evidence from cross-section data is not in conflict with our theoretical expectations. Reliable time series data are more difficult to obtain, but the available evidence provides some support for the hypothesis. For example, in a study of Colombia in the period 1950–63, I smoothed out the bi-annual coffee cycle by using a two-year moving average and then regressed domestic savings on foreign capital. I obtained the following result:[12]

$$\frac{S}{Y} = 21.5 - 0.84 \ \frac{A}{Y} \ ; \ R^2 = 0.43$$
$$(0.29)$$

In a study of Brazilian savings rates N. H. Leff found some evidence that domestic savings and foreign investment were inversely related, particularly during and immediately after the Second World War, 1940–7, although this did not seem to be the case in the later period 1947–60.[13]

Finally, in a cross-section, multiple correlation analysis covering 33 developed and underdeveloped countries over a long period (in a few cases since the mid-nineteenth century), Colin Clark found a distinct inverse relationship between domestic and foreign savings. His results suggest that a 10 per cent capital *outflow* raises the net domestic savings rate by 5.8 per cent.[14]

The results of abstract theory and simple econometrics may not prove our point; the reader is entitled to know the precise channels through which an increase in foreign capital leads to a reduction in domestic savings.[15] There are, of course, many ways of reducing savings and the methods used will change with time and vary from one place to another. All one can do here is list several of the most obvious ways in which this can occur.

First, public savings may decline; this may happen if either tax receipts fall or there is a change in the composition of government expenditure. Tax revenues will decline if (i) the government reduces taxation, or (ii) less effort is made to collect taxes, or (iii) given inflation and an inelastic tax system, tax rates are not raised periodically. Equally important, the government may respond to increased foreign capital by changing the composition of its expenditure in favour of public consumption. State capital formation may remain virtually unchanged, and be financed in effect by foreign aid, while the expansion of government expenditure is directed toward providing more public consumption, e.g. higher salaries for civil servants and teachers, increased employment on the railroads, greater social security benefits, etc.

Second, foreign capital may lower private domestic savings. The foreign capital may be channelled to private indigenous entrepreneurs via easy credit loans of industrial development banks or similar institutions. The availability of debt finance on soft terms may reduce the incentive of local investors to save. Alternatively, private foreign capital may enter the economy through participation in mixed enterprises. In this case it is probable that foreigners will supply at least some capital that indigenous entrepreneurs would have saved themselves—out of retained profits, for instance. Yet another possibility is for private foreign capital to establish wholly-owned enterprises. In this case they are likely to compete directly with local investors—and, indeed, may be granted special tax and import privileges which enable them to do so. Foreign capitalists may pre-empt the most profitable investment opportunities and the strong, direct competition faced by local investors may tend to reduce the supply of indigenous entrepreneurship and savings.

Finally, capital imports may reduce domestic savings by stimulating the consumption of importables and exportables. The increased availability of imported goods which foreign capital facilitates may lead to an increase in their consumption. Perhaps even more likely, the increased availability of foreign exchange which accompanies capital imports may induce the goverment to adopt or maintain inappropriate exchange rates or other trade policies. The consequence of these policies may be to reduce the effort devoted to exporting and to increase domestic consumption of potential export goods.

Thus in theory one should expect foreign capital to reduce domestic savings; in practice it seems to do so, and it is easy to imagine a variety of mechanisms through which this occurs.

IV.   AID AND THE OUTPUT–CAPITAL RATIO

The savings-gap model examined in the second section of this chapter implies that foreign capital raises the growth rate by the amount ak. In the third section, however, it is argued that most foreign capital supplements consumption and that only a small part is used to increase the rate of investment. Assuming that increased consumption does not increase productivity, capital imports would increase the rate of growth by much less than orthodox models suggest, viz. by $(1-\alpha)ak$, where α is the fraction of aid consumed and varies, apparently, from roughly 0.67 to over 0.80.

If this were the end of the story one might conclude that economists have been excessively optimistic about the effectiveness of aid in promoting development, but that, none the less, aid does have a small but positive contribution to make.[16] This might be a hasty and unwarranted conclusion, however. Up to this point it has been assumed that the incremental output – capital ratio is constant or at least varies independently of capital imports. The time has come to question this assumption.

Almost no research has been done on the relationship between k and a and it is possible to find arguments which imply that the association is positive, negative or zero. Nevertheless, what evidence I have seen suggests that the output – capital ratio and *public* foreign capital are inversely correlated.[17] Since public capital accounts for about two-thirds of all capital inflows, one would expect to find a loose negative association between k and a. If this in fact turns out to be the case, then it is quite possible that the slight positive effect of foreign capital in raising investment will be more than offset by a decline in the output – capital ratio, so that the growth rate actually falls. Indeed this may be the explanation why in general there appears to be no association whatever between total capital imports and the rate of growth.[18]

Given that α is quite large, it can easily be demonstrated that the effects on growth of even a large capital inflow may be completely neutralised by a small decline in the output – capital ratio. Imagine two cases, as described in Table 8.

TABLE 8

	Case 1	Case 2
s	0.12	0.12
k	1/3	0.30
a	-	0.03
α	-	2/3
g	0.04	0.039

Case 1: $g = sk$
Case 2: $g = [(1 - \alpha)a + s]k$

In Case 1, the savings rate is 12 per cent and the output – capital ratio is 1/3; this generates a growth rate of four per cent. In Case 2, the economy receives a capital inflow equivalent to three per cent of its national income. Most models would predict that the growth rate would rise to five per cent. On the other hand, if only one-third of the capital inflow adds to total investment and if the incremental output – capital ratio falls by as little as 0.03, the aggregate rate of growth will decline fractionally. Thus growth may decline despite the fact that capital imports equivalent to 25 per cent of domestic savings are available.[19]

Obviously, a crucial step in the analysis is the hypothesis that the output – capital ratio will fall as aid increases.[20] Why does this occur? One reason is the motivation of the aid donors.[21] Donor countries use aid as an instrument to achieve many objectives, among which economic development is only one. Political objectives are paramount and in most instances these can best be achieved and goodwill in the recipient country established by concentrating on large, dramatic, highly visible projects which can stand as monuments to the generosity of the donors.[22] The demand for monumental projects is likely to create its own supply, but in the process the effectiveness of investment will almost surely diminish.

Next, aid agencies have certain ideological biases against government ownership of directly productive activities. Since aid is usually channelled directly to the government of the recipient country, this ideological bias tends to alter the pattern of investment in favour of social overhead capital and economic infrastructure—transport facilities, electric energy, housing and schools. Road construction is encouraged; factory construction is discouraged. It is possible, of course, that in some countries infrastructure deserves priority, but a general bias against directly productive activities should tend to lower the aggregate output – capital ratio.

Furthermore, quite apart from motives and ideology, the administration of aid programmes may tend to lower the effectiveness of investment. If an agency is going to lend £40 million to a country it would normally prefer to finance one project costing £40 million than 40 projects costing £1 million each. By concentrating on a few large projects the agency can reduce the difficulties of supervising its projects and keep down its administrative costs. For this reason, aid programmes tend to sponsor large dams rather than small irrigation schemes, major highways rather than secondary roads, university buildings rather than village schools, etc. Again, there is no presumption that large projects have a higher rate of return than small projects. If anything, the opposite may be true, and any systematic tendency to alter the pattern of investment in favour of large schemes is likely to lower the output – capital ratio.

One of the great difficulties with project aid is that assistance normally can be used only to finance the foreign exchange costs of a project. This practice induces countries, first, to select projects which are intensive in foreign exchange and, second, to design any given project so as to maximise the foreign exchange component of total costs. This additional bias in project selection and design reduces still further the impact on growth of any given volume of investment.

Finally, there is tied aid. From the recipient's point of view tied aid tends to lead, first, to a higher cost of imported goods—since the prices of goods imported under tied-aid agreements will almost certainly be higher than world prices—and, second, to a continuing flow of high-cost imports in the form of spare parts and ancillary equipment complementary to the aid-financed imports. Thus a country may become 'locked in' to a high-cost source of supply *via* tied aid, and this might permanently lower the productivity of its investments. It certainly is not obvious that a larger volume of aid that is tied is preferable to less aid that is untied. Indeed the practice of tying aid greatly increases the costs of investment to the underdeveloped countries, lowers the aggregate output – capital ratio and reduces the international competitiveness of aid-financed activities. [23] In other words, because resources are fungible, capital imports may not increase the investment ratio very much but they may influence the composition of investment and the methods of production.

V. A DIAGRAMMATIC TREATMENT

Foreign capital may reduce the rate of growth. Whether it does so, and to what extent, depends upon whether or not capital imports A lower domestic savings S and the incremental output – capital ratio k. Some of the possibilities are illustrated in Figure 5.

The investment frontiers ff_1 and ff_2 indicate the various combinations of domestic and foreign savings that could be used to achieve a given target rate of growth g^*. The intercept on the vertical axis is determined by g^* and by the k that would prevail if all investments were financed domestically. The value of the intercept is $Y_0(g^*/k)$, where Y_0 is the initial level of income. The slope of the frontier depends on the extent to which capital imports affect the output – capital ratio. If foreign capital leaves k unaltered, the slope of the frontier will be minus 1, that is, ff_1; if k declines, the slope will be less steep, for example ff_2.

The line SS_0 is the domestic savings function. It is drawn in such a way as to suggest that domestic savings and capital imports are inversely associated, although in Figure 5 we have assumed that savings fall only moderately as aid increases.

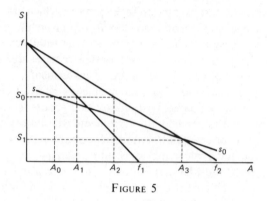

FIGURE 5

Assume that initially there is S_0 amount of domestic savings and an inflow of public and private foreign capital of A_0. According to most macro-economic aid models, additional capital imports of $A_0 A_1$ would be needed in order to achieve the growth target. If one considers the adverse impact of foreign aid on the output – capital ratio, however, a much larger aid inflow would be necessary, viz. an amount equal to $A_0 A_2$. But even this would not suffice if capital imports cause domestic savings to fall. In terms of the above diagram, $A_0 A_3$ amount of additional aid would be necessary to offset the decline in k and the fall in savings from S_0 to S_1. The growth target could still be achieved, but only if the country were nearly 'drowned' in aid. Unfortunately, as shown in Section I above, the amount of foreign assistance being provided at present is sufficient to drown or saturate only a very few countries.[24]

The conclusion reached so far is mildly optimistic: increased foreign aid lowers the effectiveness of investment, but it does supplement consumption and helps (slightly) to raise the growth rate. This 'optimistic' outcome, however, is a result of the assumption that domestic savings are only moderately sensitive to capital imports. Were a different savings function to be used the outcome would be radically different.

The savings function drawn in Figure 6 is a more accurate representation of the statistical evidence presented earlier. If most foreign assistance is used to supplement consumption and if capital imports alter the pattern of investment and thereby lower the output – capital ratio, it is possible that no amount of additional foreign aid will enable a country to achieve a given growth objective. Indeed, in this 'pessimistic' case a reduction in capital imports will increase the growth rate and enable a country to achieve its objective, whereas an increase in capital

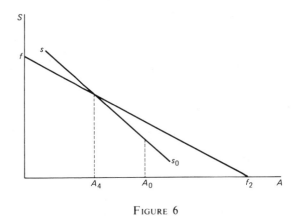

FIGURE 6

imports will retard growth. In terms of Figure 6, the required reduction in foreign capital inflow is equal to $A_4 A_0$. This might be called a negative resource gap.

In other words, under some conditions a reduction in foreign capital might lead to an increase in the domestic savings ratio and a rise in the incremental output – capital ratio. These two effects might more than compensate for the reduction in total available resources and, as a result, the rate of economic development might actually increase. The cost of self-reliance, however, would be some reduction in the level of current consumption. That is, contrary to what is often alleged, the 'price' of economic independence may not be slower growth but less current consumption.

NOTES AND REFERENCES

1. OECD, *Development Assistance 1968 and Recent Trends*, (Paris: 1969).
2. The recent custom of calculating the 'grant element' in loans by discounting the repayment stream at 10 per cent and subtracting this from the face value of the loan merely obscures the trends in foreign aid. Obviously if a high enough discount rate is used almost any loan can be made to appear as if it is essentially a grant.
3. See Keith Griffin, *Underdevelopment in Spanish America* (London: Allen and Unwin, 1969). Ch. III.
4. The most frequently cited model is that of Professor Chenery. See H. B. Chenery and A. Strout, 'Foreign Assistance and Economic Development', *American Economic Review* (Sep. 1966) and the bibliography at the end of that article. Also see R. F. Mikesell, *The Economics of Foreign Aid* (London: Weidenfeld and Nicolson, 1968) Ch. 3.

5. If this hypothesis is correct one would expect to find a positive association between *a* and *s*. It will be shown below that the association is usually inverse.

6. See Arjun Sengupta, 'Foreign Capital Requirements for Economic Development', *Oxford Economic Papers*, Mar. 1968. In 12 out of 31 countries studied by Chenery and Strout (op. cit., Table A-1), the marginal propensity was less than the average propensity to save $(s' < s)$!

7. If a foreign exchange gap exists a simple regression of ΔI on ΔA should produce a regression coefficient ≥ 1 (it would be unity only if $n = 1$), and a regression of ΔS on ΔA should produce a regression coefficient > 0, where I and S refer to the level of investment and savings respectively.

8. Op. cit., Ch. II.

9. See, for example, H. W. Singer, 'External Aid: For Plans or Projects?' *Economic Journal* (Sep. 1965).

10. This possibility is mentioned by Professor Leontieff in 'A Theoretical Note on Time Preference, Productivity of Capital, Stagnation and Economic Growth', *American Economic Review* (Mar. 1958).

11. Inter-American Committee for the Alliance for Progress, Organization of American States, *La Brecha Externa de la America Latina 1968–1973* (Washington: Dec. 1968) p. 30.

12. See Keith Griffin, *Land Concentration and Rural Poverty* (London: Macmillan, 1976) Ch. 3.

13. N. H. Leff, 'Marginal Saving Rates in the Development Process: the Brazilian Experience', *Economic Journal* (Sep. 1968) pp. 615–16.

14. Colin Clark, *Population Growth and Land Use* (London: Macmillan, 1967) p. 268.

15. The regression equations could be interpreted in a variety of ways. For example, one could claim that the equations are incorrectly specified and provide evidence for an investment function. Alternatively, it could be argued that the line of causation should be reversed: countries receive aid *because* they save a low proportion of their national income. This last interpretation, however, clearly is wrong, as even a cursory examination of the motives for aid will show.

16. One might also conclude that since aid is not significantly increasing the productive capacity of the recipient economy, out of which repayment of debts should occur, grants rather than loans should be offered. It is doubtful that the interests of a country are served by encouraging it to incur future repayment obligations if it is known that the means for discharging the obligations are unlikely to exist.

17. See Keith Griffin, *Land Concentration and Rural Povery*, Ch. 6; Keith Griffin, *Underdevelopment in Spanish America* (London: Allen and Unwin, 1969) Ch. III.

18. The lack of association between aid and development is accepted now by most observers. Even the Pearson Report confesses that 'the correlation between the amounts of aid received in the past decades and the growth performance is very weak' (*Partners in Development* (London: Pall Mall Press, 1969) p. 49.). Yet the Commissioners—a group of eight politicians, financiers and economists—insist that foreign aid 'has been of *first* importance in the psychology of development'. (Ibid., pp. 51–2; emphasis

added.) No evidence for this statement is provided and, as far as I can tell, none of the 27 staff members or two dozen consultants employed by the Commission is a psychologist.

19. In Case 2, the domestic savings rate declines *ex post* to 0.10, i.e. $0.12 + 0.03 (1 - 2/3) - 0.03$. Donor countries may then claim that foreign capital supplements domestic savings and the growth rate by 30 per cent. This claim, as has been shown, may be utter nonsense.

20. A simple test of the hypothesis would be to regress k on A/I. If the hypothesis is correct the regression coefficient should be negative.

21. Motives, as well as some other issues raised in this chapter, are discussed in a tentative way in Keith Griffin and John Enos, 'Foreign Assistance: Objectives and Consequences', *Economic Development and Cultural Change* (Apr. 1970).

22. This does not imply, of course, that the governments of some underdeveloped countries do not favour monumental projects for reasons of their own.

23. About 75 per cent of all bilateral assistance is tied. UNCTAD studies suggest that the direct excess cost of tied aid to recipient countries was roughly 10 to 15 per cent in Iran, 20 per cent in Tunisia and 12.4 per cent in Chile. (UNCTAD TD/7/Supp. 8, 21 Nov. 1967, 'The Costs of Aid-Tying to Recipient Countries'). Haq's study of Pakistan indicates excess costs of 12 to 51 per cent (M. ul Haq, 'Tied Credits – a Quantitative Analysis', in J. H. Adler, ed., *Capital Movements and Economic Development*, London: Macmillan, 1967) and J. Bhagwati estimates that in general excess cost may be as high as 49.3 per cent ('The tying of aid', UNCTAD, TD/7/Supp. 4, 1968).

24. The 'total net official flow' of foreign assistance in the period 1964–7 was equivalent to 2.2 per cent of the GDP of the underdeveloped countries. The figure in Jordan was 14.8 per cent, in Papua and New Guinea 29.1 per cent, and in Laos 33.9 per cent. (*Partners in Development*, pp. 392–3.)

Appendix to Chapter 3.
Foreign capital: a reply
to some critics

There are a great many people who in principle would favour a redistribution of income from rich to poor nations. I count myself among them. At this level of generality my critics and I are all on the side of the angels. In practice, however, we differ, and I have come to the reluctant conclusion that 'capital imports, rather than accelerating development, have in some cases retarded it'.[1] Frances Stewart, Charles Kennedy and A. P. Thirlwall, in their Comments, contest this statement but provide no empirical evidence. What, then, are the facts?

M. Kellman, in the course of criticising one of my articles, has supplied recent evidence that foreign capital does not seem to have promoted growth.[2] He measures aid dependence by the ratio of bilateral plus multilateral aid A to total imports M, and finds that the rate of growth of income during 1960–5 was inversely associated with A/M in both a 40-country sample and in a 12-country sample of Latin American nations. Moreover, in a regression of the rate of growth of *per capita* income on A/M, he obtained a negative association in Latin America and a barely positive association (0.01) in the 40-country sample. Thus the hypothesis that aid promotes growth would appear to be untrue whether we look at Latin America alone or at the underdeveloped world as a whole, whether growth is measured net or gross of population increase, and whether dependence is measured as the ratio of aid to imports or, as I have done elsewhere, as aid to income. If nothing else, we should be able to agree that there is a problem to be explained.

Part of the explanation why aid has not led to faster development is that it is not designed for this purpose. That is, the major purpose of aid is to further the interests of the donors rather than those of the recipients. This is hardly a sufficient explanation, however. Growth, after all, could be a by-product of policies designed for other purposes. I argue that there are theoretical and practical reasons why this is

74

unlikely. My critics do not agree. I propose, in what follows, to discuss our major points of disagreement under four headings: the definition of domestic savings, the role of capital imports in supplementing consumption, the effect of foreign aid on the pattern of investment, and the extent to which capital imports alleviate or aggravate balance of payments difficulties.

I. THE DEFINITION OF SAVINGS

Economists are accustomed to thinking that aggregate consumption depends, among other things, upon national income. In a world in which capital transfers occur, however, it is reasonable to assume that consumption will be a positive function of total available resources, i.e. national income plus net capital imports. Especially when capital transfers are firmly expected, they will be treated as part of total income when expenditure decisions are made. Unanticipated capital transfers will be treated as transitory phenomena and may be largely saved, but in the case of anticipated capital transfers the normal marginal propensity to consume will apply. If this is accepted, it follows as surely as night follows day that—unless the marginal propensity to consume is zero— capital imports will raise total consumption and reduce domestic savings.

Assume that our consumption function is of the form

$$C = d + \alpha(Y + A) \tag{1}$$

Since $S = Y - C$ by definition, it follows that

$$S = -d + \beta Y - \alpha A \tag{2}$$

where $\beta = 1 - \alpha$. In other words, given the *level* of income, the larger the inflow of capital the lower the *level* of domestic savings. Equation (2) can be written in ratio form. The easiest way to do this is to suppress the intercept and divide through by Y:

$$\frac{S}{Y} = \beta - \alpha\frac{A}{Y} \tag{3}$$

Equation (3) does not imply a constant level of income; it tells ùs that the higher the *ratio* of aid to income the smaller will be the *rate* of domestic savings. Failure to understand this simple point is the cause of much confusion in Mr Eshag's Comment on my essay.[3]

Most of the cross-section regressions I presented were similar to

Equation (3). Time series equations rather similar to Equation (2) have also been run, however.[4] The results confirm my expectations.

A hasty reader of Mrs Stewart's note may receive the impression that the decline in domestic savings is merely a semantic trick, i.e. 'that domestic savings will fall because of the way they are defined'. This is not true. The definition of domestic savings S I have used is identical to that employed by national income satisticians, viz. the difference between total net investment I and the surplus of imports M over exports X. The import surplus is, of course, equal to the net inflow of foreign capital A.[5]

$$S \equiv I - (M - X) \equiv I - A$$

Mr Eshag makes a rather different point from those we have considered so far. He claims that 'in the great majority' of under-developed countries 'there exists not only a substantial reservoir of unemployed labour resources but also varying amounts of unutilised land and equipment which could often be put to use . . . but for the presence of foreign exchange constraint . . .'. Yet he fails to explain why under such circumstances the economy is unable to earn or save foreign exchange, and thereby overcome the constraint, by implementing policies of import controls, tariffs, export subsidies, devaluation and the like. Mr Eshag's views are the reverse of my own. He argues that 'there is in fact every reason to expect that domestic savings will increase' as a result of foreign aid. Given his assumptions it is, of course, true that the rise in savings due to the multiplier may counteract the fall due to consumption out of aid. I have no quarrel with his algebra, but I do dispute his economics. The evidence I have seen tends to support my interpretation. If Mr Eshag has better evidence I would certainly like to see it.

II. CAPITAL IMPORTS AND CONSUMPTION

Our results, and those of others, e.g. Thomas Weisskopf, are quite clear: capital imports tend to supplement consumption as well as investment, and models which predict or assume that all resource transfers from abroad will be used to accelerate capital accumulation are likely to exaggerate the impact of capital imports on investment and growth.

This does not imply that a rise in consumption is undesirable. Indeed, in so far as capital imports permit a more egalitarian distribution of consumption in the world, they are to be welcomed. On this point, Mrs Stewart, Professor Kennedy, Mr Thirlwall and I are in agreement.

The 'ambivalent, and even inconsistent, attitude' which Kennedy and Thirlwall detect stems from my doubt that in practice capital imports have been used to reduce inequality. For example, in Pakistan, a major aid recipient, *per capita* income has been rising quite rapidly for about a decade. Moreover, between 1963–4 and 1969–70 the share of consumption in GNP increased by nearly two and a half per cent. At the same time, the *per capita* availability of food grains has remained roughly constant and the *per capita* availability of cotton cloth and other wage goods has declined. In other words, the consumption of the poor declined, whereas that of the rich increased. Thus before one argues that foreign aid improves the distribution of consumption goods one needs to have much more evidence as to precisely whose consumption is increased by capital imports.

The three critics mentioned above note that some forms of consumption may help to raise productivity, and Mrs Stewart cites a passage in one of my books to the same effect, but she then chides me for largely ignoring the point in my discussion of the role of capital imports. The major reason why I did so is that there is little evidence that capital imports have financed an increase in consumption of those specific goods which would accelerate development. The most probable exception to this statement is the provision of food supplies under the American P.L.480 programme. Yet it is far from certain that even this aid programme contributed to a net long-run increase in *per capita* food consumption. It is quite possible that in several important countries, e.g. India, food aid enabled the government to neglect agriculture and turn its attention elsewhere, with the result that domestic production increased more slowly than would otherwise have been the case.

Generally speaking, it appears unlikely that additional consumption will raise the productivity of labour unless the increased consumption is directed largely toward the poorest groups in the community. In other words, if the increased consumption which capital imports finance is to accelerate development, two conditions must be satisified: first, aggregate consumption of specific items must increase (e.g. animal proteins); and second, these items must be distributed to groups where their impact on productivity will be maximised. If capital imports enable the rich to drive more Mercedes, they will not accelerate growth; if they enable the poor to improve their diet, enjoy better health and have smaller families, they may make a significant contribution.

III.   AID AND THE PATTERN OF INVESTMENT

Several of my critics seem to have misunderstood what I was trying to say about the relationship between capital imports and the effectiveness of investment. My views are easily summarised. First, capital imports do not lead to a significant increase in total investment. Thus the net addition of foreign capital to other investment efforts is slight. Second, a project financed by foreign aid is likely to have a higher capital – output ratio than the same project financed by domestic savings. Because of tied aid, a low nominal cost of capital, and a preference of donors to finance only the foreign exchange costs of assisted projects, an aid-financed scheme is likely to use resources less efficiently than a domestically-financed scheme. Third, and most important, a country which relies heavily on foreign aid is likely to have a completely different set of investment projects from one which relies on domestic savings to finance development.

Whenever the preferences of donors for projects differ from those of recipients, foreign aid agencies may alter the pattern of investment without affecting the total very much. Suppose, for example, that in the absence of capital imports a country would undertake a £200 million investment programme consisting of a fertiliser plant, a series of small factories producing pumps for tubewells and a flour mill. Assume that the incremental capital – output ratio (ICOR) for these projects is 4, so that output rises by £50 million in the first instance. Alternatively, the country may be able to obtain £60 million of foreign aid tied, say, to investment in a large dam, an atomic energy station and a super-highway. As we have seen, consumption is likely to rise by approximately two-thirds of this aid, so that total investment is unlikely to rise to more than £220 million. If the ICOR on this larger set of projects is higher than 4.4, the inflow of aid will cause a decline in the rate of growth of output.

In some cases foreign aid may finance the marginal project and leave all other projects unchanged. More frequently, however, the donors are able to pre-empt domestic resources and alter the entire investment programme, thereby substituting their preferences for those of the recipient government. When aid 'leverage' is used in this way it is almost certain to affect the aggregate ICOR. The hypothesis put forward in Chapter 3 is that it would raise it.

IV. THE BALANCE OF PAYMENTS BURDEN

In Chapter 3 I argued that in the long run the foreign exchange gap is a pseudo-gap.[6] None of my critics refutes this proposition, although Mr Eshag describes it as 'highly doubtful' and all four claim that, in the short run, capital imports can alleviate a foreign exchange constraint. I agree that in the short run, i.e. a period during which the economy is unable to reallocate resources, additional foreign exchange may enable a country to increase investment at a much lower cost than would otherwise be possible. Before one uses this as a justification for aid, however, it is important to consider the long-run consequences.

One of the important facts of the contemporary world economy is the growing number of underdeveloped countries that are unable to service their foreign debt. Many of the largest aid recipients, in fact, have had to renegotiate their debts, some more than once. Argentina and Indonesia have rescheduled their external debt three times; Turkey, Brazil and Ghana, twice; Chile, India and Peru, once.[7] How does the two-gap model, or any other model, account for this? It doesn't, and the reason it doesn't is because it is assumed that capital imports are productively used and generate a surplus out of which the debt can be serviced. If this assumption were relaxed the facts could readily be explained.

Using the same notation as in Chapter 3, assume a country receives a net capital inflow of A and invests a certain fraction of it $(1 - \alpha)$. Ignoring the possible effects of increased consumption on the productivity of labour, and assuming an incremental output – capital ratio of k, foreign capital will raise total output by $A(1 - \alpha)k$. Interest r must be paid on the entire loan, however, not just on that part which is invested. If

$$A(1 - \alpha)k < rA$$

the additional output generated by capital imports will be insufficient to service the debt.

Countries which are forced to borrow at relatively high rates of interest and yet have a strong tendency to consume a large proportion of their capital imports may well find that their repayment obligations exceed the value of extra output produced. For example, if $\alpha = 0.8$ and $k = 0.3$, the balance of payments effects of foreign borrowing will be negative if $r > 0.06$.

The above illustration is unrealistic, however, because it is assumed that part of the capital import is consumed but that all of the additional output can be saved. In practice, some fraction of the additional income will be consumed, say α again. It is only out of the rest that debts can be serviced. In these circumstances, a country will encounter debt-servicing problems even if the rate of interest is quite low. Specifically, the balance of payments effects will be unfavourable if

$$(1 - \alpha)^2 k < r$$

If α and k have the same values as assumed in the previous paragraph, repayment obligations will exceed additional savings unless the rate of interest is no higher than 1.2 per cent. The country will then appear to have a foreign exchange constraint, and some observers may attribute this to a 'transformation problem', but in fact the difficulty is caused by a combination of excessive consumption and insufficiently productive investment.

It should be evident from these examples that even if the balance of payments is a constraint on long-run growth, capital imports may make matters worse rather than better unless (i) the government has firm control over the level of consumption, (ii) investment is allocated efficiently, and (iii) the rates of interest on foreign borrowing are low. If conditions (i) and (ii) are fulfilled, capital imports will be unnecessary, although they should be welcomed on grounds of equity. If the first two conditions are not fulfilled, capital imports other than grants create more problems than they solve.

NOTES AND REFERENCES

1. Ch. 3, p. 58.
2. M. Kellman, 'Foreign Assistance: Objectives and Consequences – Comment', *Economic Development and Cultural Change* (Oct. 1971).
3. Eprime Eshag, 'Comment', *Bulletin of the Oxford University Institute of Economics and Statistics* (May 1971).
4. See Thomas Weisskopf, 'The Impact of Foreign Capital Inflow on Domestic Savings in Underdeveloped Countries', *Journal of International Economics* (Feb. 1972).
5. At several points Mrs Stewart seems to have confused domestic savings with total net investment and national income with the flow of total available resources. See, for example, p. 141 of her comment in the *Bulletin of the Oxford University Institute of Economics and Statistics* (May 1971).
6. The assumptions underlying the foreign exchange gap are ably analysed by Vijay Joshi, 'Saving and Foreign Exchange Constraints', in P. P. Streeten (ed.), *Unfashionable Economics: Essays in Honour of Lord Balogh* (London: Weidenfeld and Nicolson, 1970).
7. Lester B. Pearson, *Partners in Development*, Table 20, pp. 383–4.

4. On the emigration of the peasantry

Political events and economic analysis have recently coincided in a remarkable way. Britain, continental Europe, Canada and the USA have all in the last few years introduced policies to restrict mass immigration. Virtually at the same time, some social scientists have begun to argue that mass emigration may not be advantageous to the underdeveloped countries. Thus, if the analysis is correct, we have a happy coincidence: what is in the political interest of the rich countries is also in the economic interest of the poor countries.

It is widely accepted, of course, that the emigration of professional and highly skilled personnel, the so-called brain drain, can have harmful effects on the growth of poor countries and the distribution of income.[1] What is now being claimed, however, is that the migration of ordinary working people is or may be detrimental to development. In its mid-term review of the progress achieved during the Second United Nations Development Decade, the International Labour Office put forward this claim in the following way:

> Until well into the 1960s it was taken for granted that the massive outflow of workers from the developing areas around the Mediterranean basin was beneficial in that it relieved unemployment and brought in much-needed foreign currency through remittances. This view is now challenged. Doubts are expressed with regard not only to the relief of unemployment but also to the beneficial nature of remittances. Though temporarily relieving the existing unemployment situation, emigration does in fact leave gaps in both agricultural and (more importantly) industrial labour supplies. It can induce cost-push inflation, lead to productivity and output losses and cause new unemployment or underemployment . . .

> While remittances are welcome in terms of the balance of payments, they have at least two detrimental effects which makes their net effect

81

questionable: first, their receipt may turn significant numbers of agricultural producers into consumers, which decreases both the domestic food supply and the surplus to be set aside for exports; and second, the inflow of purchasing power creates excess demand in inelastic supply conditions, and this leads directly to demand-pull inflation and indirectly to cost-push inflationary pressure, with corresponding effects on the balance of payments.[2]

The series of allegations against migration quoted above has been discussed at greater length in an article published in the *International Labour Review*[3] and reiterated in a 'Working Paper' issued by the World Employment Programme.[4] There is thus a danger that these views will become accepted merely as a result of repetition.

In my opinion these allegations are almost entirely false. The migration of ordinary working people to higher-paid jobs abroad, whenever feasible, is in principle a major avenue of escape from poverty and oppression. The restrictive immigration policies of rich countries clearly are contrary to the interests of poor people in underdeveloped countries and it is misleading to suggest the reverse, or to imply that there might be a case for underdeveloped countries to erect further obstacles.

In the analysis which follows I shall concentrate on the migration of unskilled labour, and particularly on the emigration of country folk, or on what Latin Americans call *campesinos*. One reason for concentrating on such people is that most migrants are of rural origin, although many may have resided in an urban area during the period immediately preceding emigration. Even in Turkey, one of the few countries with massive emigration from the cities, a survey conducted by the State Planning Organization in 1971 revealed that 50 per cent of the migrants were from rural areas and 43 per cent were residing in a village before their departure.[5]

Another reason for concentrating on rural migrants is that one can thereby scrutinise several of the specific allegations that are made against emigration. In particular, we shall want to examine the claims that migration turns 'agricultural producers into consumers', lowers the productivity of labour, reduces the supply of food and exports, leaves 'gaps' in the labour force and produces inflation. In addition, we shall discuss the effects of massive emigration on the distribution of income.

Let us begin by examining the effects of rural emigration on food production or, more generally, on agricultural output as a whole.

I. PRODUCTION AND WELFARE

The outflow of unskilled rural workers, whom I shall call peasants[6] for short, can have direct and indirect effects on the total supply of agricultural labour. Let us start by considering the direct effects. First, if the emigrants are permanently unemployed in their country of origin, an unlikely assumption, or if there is surplus labour in the sense used by A. K. Sen,[7] the withdrawal of one peasant reduces the available labour force directly by one man-year but has no effect on labour inputs used in agriculture. Emigration raises the welfare both of the migrant and of those left behind who otherwise would have had to provide him with subsistence. Unemployment or surplus labour decline marginally while output remains unchanged.

Second, if the emigrants are fully employed, and there is no surplus labour, the withdrawal of one peasant reduces both the labour force and labour inputs by one man-year. Agricultural output declines by an amount equivalent to the marginal product of labour. The income of the migrant rises, however, as do the incomes of the remaining members of the family. If the extended family system predominates in rural areas, the number of beneficiaries may be quite large. The amount by which the combined income of the migrant and his extended family increases depends on the difference between the wage income actually received abroad w, and m, the marginal product of labour in agriculture, which often will be low and in very extreme cases may tend toward zero.[8]

The division of this increased income ($w - m$) between the migrant and the extended family depends on the value of remittances r and the annual consumption of the peasant prior to migration c. Under some assumptions the latter would be approximately equal to the average product of labour, but for the purposes of our analysis there is no need to specify its value. We thus have the following results:

(i) $w - m$ = rise in total income;
(ii) $w - r - c$ = rise in migrant's income;
(iii) $c - m + r$ = rise in extended family's income.

Irrespective of what happens to agricultural production, provided only that $w > m$,[9] the direct effects of emigration clearly raise welfare; everybody benefits and in principle nobody loses. Moreover, this may be true whether or not the emigrant remits money to his extended family.[10] In fact, as long as the average consumption of the peasantry exceeds the marginal product of labour ($c > m$), it pays the family to subsidise the migration of a worker.[11] While as long as the wage received abroad exceeds the peasant's consumption at home ($w > c$), the emigrant can send some funds home without sacrificing his own standard of living. Hence the value of remittances and their direction of flow are indeterminate $(r \gtrless 0)$ although one would expect to find an upper (positive) and lower (negative) limit to remittances:

$$(m-c) \leq r \leq w-c).$$

The majority of writers implicitly assume that emigrants remit money home, i.e. that $r > 0$. Given that we are concerned with the migration of labour from the rural sector of underdeveloped countries to the industrial and service sectors of developed countries, this assumption probably is correct in the majority of cases, although it may not be valid universally. For example, there may be frequent instances where it does not apply to rural – urban migration within an underdeveloped country.

Let us assume, however, that the migrant does in fact send money home. It has then been argued that because of these remittances the supply of labour in rural areas may be reduced *indirectly* when remaining family members become unwilling to till their own fields or those of their landlord . . .'. This occurs because 'where the breadwinner remits sizeable sums, the need to ensure one's subsistence through work diminishes, and inactivity or the life of a mere consumer becomes possible or even desirable'.[12]

Two questions arise from these statements. First, are they correct? Second, does it matter?

Imagine for a moment that the extended family we are considering works on a small parcel of land. By varying the intensity of effort, e.g. the number of hours worked per 'day', the members of the household are able to choose collectively between goods and leisure. In Figure 7, if the family does no work at all, it can enjoy T hours of leisure, whereas if it devotes all its available time to work, it can enjoy G_1 quantity of goods. The line $G_1 T$ indicates the various combinations of goods and leisure open to the household.[13] Presumably the combination yielding the greatest welfare, say E_1, will be selected. (Readers who are so inclined can imagine an indifference curve tangential to $G_1 T$ at E_1.) At this point OL leisure is enjoyed and OQ goods are produced and consumed as a result of LT amount of work.

If a relative or friend resident abroad suddenly were to begin to send remittances equal to OR, the consumption-frontier would be vertically displaced by this amount, to $G_2 t$. Which of the new combinations of goods and leisure available to the household would be selected cannot be predicted in the absence of knowledge about household preferences. It certainly is possible that a combination such as E_2 would be chosen,

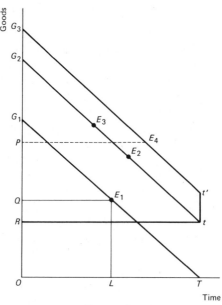

FIGURE 7

implying an increase in leisure and a corresponding reduction in work and output. This must be the case envisaged by those who believe remittances convert 'significant numbers of agricultural producers into consumers'. It also is possible, however, that a position such as E_3 would be selected. In this case, contrary to the critics of migration, leisure time would diminish and there would be a corresponding increase in work and output. Thus it is not obvious that emigrants' remittances would indirectly reduce the amount of effort supplied.

The presumption so far, however, is that they would. Unless leisure is an 'inferior' activity, one would expect hours of work to fall in response to lump-sum transfers of income. This does not imply, however, that the reduction in employment and output is a reflection of, or is in any way associated with, a decline in welfare. On the contrary, welfare unambiguously increases, both because measured income and the volume of consumption are higher and because the amount of leisure is greater. The fact that output or GDP falls—if it does—is irrelevant; income and the welfare of the household have increased.[14]

Moreover, there is no basis whatever for claiming that this process can 'lead to productivity . . . losses'.[15] The possible direct and indirect reduction of employed labour consequent upon emigration and the receipt of remittances will result in an increase in the average and marginal productivity of labour. The reason for this is that a reduction in labour inputs, *ceteris paribus*, will be associated with a rise in the amount of land (and fixed capital) per employed person. The more favourable land – man ratio will lead to higher productivity of labour, although the volume of production and yields per hectare will be lower.

The greater relative scarcity of labour and higher output per man-day are likely to be translated into higher wage rates for landless labourers. This, in turn, assuming the substitution effect of a wage increase is larger than the income effect, may induce an increase in the amount of effort labourers are willing to supply. To the extent that this occurs, higher wages will partially counteract the possible tendency for migration and remittances to reduce output.

More significant is likely to be the effect of remittances on increasing capital formation and hence output in rural areas. We know that migrants save an extraordinarily high proportion of their income. In Turkey, for example, rural migrants saved 39 per cent of their income on average and remitted 15 per cent, the rest being retained in the host country.[16] Unfortunately, almost nothing is known about what proportion of income from remittances is saved and invested by the peasant household. There is no reason to assume, however, as the critics of migration implicitly do, that income transfers from abroad are devoted exclusively to consumption. On the contrary, general theoretical reasoning plus evidence from macro-economic studies of foreign capital inflows suggest that resource transfers do accelerate the rate of capital accumulation, even if only slightly.[17]

This being so, one would expect migration to lead to a rise in investment per hectare and per man. The effect of this, in terms of Figure 7, would be to displace $G_2 t$ further to the right, say, to $G_3 t'$, where $G_2 G_3$ is the rise in production and income due to investment out of remittances. Given that capital is very scarce in the rural areas of almost all underdeveloped countries, the rate of return on investment should be high, and the consequent rise in total output, yields and labour productivity should be sufficient to offset any tendency there may be for output to fall as a result of greater leisure.[18] Indeed, in my judgement the processes that have been described, far from reducing output in rural areas, are more likely to increase it.

II. THE DISTRIBUTION OF INCOME

In most countries the emigration of the peasantry has been a marginal phenomenon and the analysis of its effects can be confined to the welfare of the migrant peasant and his extended family. Everyone else can be ignored. There are a few cases, however, notably in the Caribbean and in some Mediterranean countries, where a substantial movement of the peasantry out of agriculture and into the industrial and service sectors of North America and Europe has occurred. In cases such as these the effects of emigration are likely to spread quite widely throughout the economy.

One such effect concerns the distribution of income. If the rate of out-migration exceeds the natural rate of growth of the labour force in rural areas, the supply of labour will tend to decline. This, in turn, for any given rate of growth of demand for labour, will tend to push up wage rates. More generally, if emigration is large enough to produce excess demand for labour at the original wage, there will be a tendency for wage rates to rise. As a result of higher wages, assuming the elasticity of substitution is less than one, the share of labour in total agricultural income will also rise, and there will be a corresponding fall in the share of profits and landlord rents. Thus, provided the migrants are poor, unskilled peasants, emigration from rural areas is likely to result in a more equal distribution of income.

This benefit to the peasantry from emigration is additional to the other gains that have been identified. That is, there are four sources of benefit. First, the migrant benefits directly from the higher wages obtainable abroad, provided only that $w > c$. Second, the remaining members of the family benefit indirectly, assuming $c > m$. Third, they benefit directly if $r > c$, and this benefit will be compounded if the propensity to save out of remittances is positive. Finally, assuming that the migratory flows are non-marginal, other peasant households benefit from the tendency of m (and hence rural wages) to rise. The only losers are large landowners who farm their land with peasant labour and, to the extent that urban wages increase, the capitalist class in the cities. The reduction in the power of the property-owning classes and the improvement in the distribution of income which massive emigration entails should be counted as an important social gain.

The analysis so far, however, has tended to ignore the heterogeneity of the rural working classes. The peasantry is not a homogeneous social category and it could be argued that emigration is not random but systematically favours particular groups in rural areas in such a way as to accentuate social differences and economic inequality within the working population. For instance, the costs of movement and infor-mation may discriminate against the very poor and favour those who come from relatively prosperous households—the larger village traders and shopkeepers, artisans who have amassed a bit of capital, the sons of landowners. In so far as poverty itself reduces mobility, the social composition of the supply of emigrants may include a disproportionate number of gentry and other more advantaged persons. Moreover, there may be economic forces on the demand side which strengthen these tendencies. For example, differences in the pressure of demand for various types of workers in the receiving countries may favour, say, the young and the more enterprising or immigrants who have at least a secondary education or those who are highly skilled.

These rather subtle processes could result in a drain of 'human capital' from rural areas, and the loss of talent and skills could be of sufficient magnitude to affect adversely the well-being of those left behind. Even if the loss of 'human capital' is not massive, the departure of persons with essential skills or aptitudes could inflict hardship on non-migrants by leaving large 'gaps' in the labour force. For example, the emigration of the village baker could deprive the rest of the community of the 'staff of life'.

The 'gap' analysis is plausible, however, only if the gaps remain unfilled. Bread could be purchased from a neighbouring village, housewives could make their own bread, or, perhaps more likely, someone could take advantage of the opportunity created by the emigrant and set himself up in business as a village baker. It is possible that in most cases the village skills lost through emigration could be replaced quickly, particularly if the emigrant leaves behind the tools of his trade, disposing of them through sale, rental or gift. In other words, the elasticity of supply of 'skilled' rural workers may be much greater than is presupposed in the gap analysis.

Unfortunately, little empirical evidence is available on these issues, but the information collected by the survey in Turkey, referred to above, does not suggest to this observer that the problem of a skill drain is serious enough to justify governments controlling or restricting the emigration of the peasantry. Statements to the effect that the balance of advantage is 'too uncertain to justify a continuation of unregulated outflows'[19] rest on weak theoretical and factual foundations. Apparently, most of the rural migrants from Turkey are not well educated: in 1971, in fact, 97 per cent of the emigrants had only a primary education or less.[20] Most migrants (73 per cent) were classified as unskilled workers; a small number (2 per cent) were unemployed and an equally small number were semi-skilled.[21] These 77 per cent of rural migrants must surely have come from among the poorest groups in the country and it is difficult to imagine that their departure increased inequality in the distribution of income.

Evidently this whole subject deserves closer study—one can conclude little on the basis of one country's experience—but pending strong counter-evidence the presumption should be that the emigration of the peasantry probably reduces inequality and that this is one of several mechanisms which tends to raise the income of the rural poor.

III. INFLATION AND THE BALANCE OF TRADE

It has been claimed that the emigration of the rural labour force can have negative secondary effects which can outweigh the positive effects we have emphasised. Since these effects are likely to be more prominent, the larger the migratory flow, let us consider an extreme and rather absurd case.

Assume that the entire rural labour force of, say, Turkey, N persons, emigrates with their dependants and receives a real income in, say, West Germany that is five times higher than average consumption prior to migration;[22] assume also that one-fifth of this income is remitted to Turkey, the entire population of which is now in urban areas. In terms of our previous notation, $w = 5c$ and $r = 0.2w$. The rise in the total income of emigrants, therefore, is $N(5c - c - c) = 3cN$. That is, income rises 200 per cent. Gross domestic product, of course, falls by a proportion equivalent to the share of rural activities in total output,[23] but this has no welfare significance for the approximately 75 per cent of the Turkish population who are today classified as rural.

The urban (or U) population of Turkey – approximately 25 per cent of the total—also would benefit. The rise in total urban incomes would be $N(0.2w)$, or Nc. This sum, when distributed over the non-migrant population would raise their *per capita* income by Nc/U, or $3c$. That is, each urban resident would receive from his emigrant peasant kinsman a remittance equal to three times the annual consumption of a peasant before migration. Purely by chance, this is identical to the rise in peasant incomes. A pretty good bonus for those who stay at home!

Sceptics claim to detect social costs lurking behind the *ceteris paribus* clause which offset these enormous private benefits. First, it is argued that remittances 'tend to fuel money supply and therefore inflation'.[24] Exactly how this is supposed to happen, however, is not explained. Normally one would expect that gifts of convertible foreign currency would reduce the rate of price increase rather than the reverse. Moreover, even if inflation were to accelerate, the connection between changes in the level of prices and changes in welfare is unclear.

A uniform rise in all prices would leave unaltered our conclusions about the effects on welfare of emigrants' remittances. The reason for this is that the analysis has been conducted in terms of changes in real income rather than in money incomes. On the other hand, it might be thought that inflation would be accompanied by a change in relative commodity prices, and not just by equi-proportionate changes in all prices. In the limiting case of a small, fully-open economy, the relative prices of goods entering into international trade would be unaffected by variations in domestic production and demand, since such a country would be a 'price taker'. Hence the argument clearly does not apply to freely traded goods in small countries. It is true, however, that the relative price of non-tradeable goods such as land and buildings could rise. Moreover, in countries which are large enough to influence the prices at which they buy and sell internationally, even the relative price of tradeables could change. It is most unlikely, however, that the quantitative significance of the welfare loss (or gain) arising from changes in relative prices would be other than minute.

A second social cost attributed to emigration and remittances concerns the balance of payments. It requires mental gymnastics to transform a gift of foreign exchange into a factor which harms a country's external payments. No one has yet achieved this feat, but the ILO hints darkly that because of lower exports and higher imports induced by inflation the net effects are 'questionable'.[25] Even in our extreme example, however, it is far from clear that the exodus of the peasantry leads to a deterioration in the country's payments position. From that example we know only that 75 per cent of the population emigrates and that consequently all exports originating in rural areas disappear. In the case of Turkey this means that total exports would decline by 70 per cent. What happens to the balance of trade (before taking remittances into account) then depends upon the urban population's propensity to import and the proportion of income spent on imports by the peasantry before migration. No doubt an illustration could be concocted in which a trade deficit appeared, and if necessary this could be corrected by a depreciation of the exchange rate. It is more probable, however, that an inflow of remittances would make de-valuation unnecessary. Indeed an appreciation of the exchange rate is more likely than the reverse.

The reallocation of relatively unskilled labour which mass emigration represents contributes to greater efficiency in resource utilisation and a rise in world output. Migration induced by the expectation of higher incomes abroad is, therefore, entirely consistent with the principle of comparative advantage. Moreover, this remains true even if migration were to result in the total abandonment of some economic activities, as in our extreme and hypothetical example of Turkish agriculture. Only if the marginal social product of labour in the country of emigration were higher than the marginal social product of labour in the country of immigration would migration lead to diminished output and efficiency and a violation of the principle of comparative advantage. While 'distortions' in the labour market undoubtedly exist, and can in theory produce an inefficient allocation of labour, especially through excessive rural-to-urban migration within a single country, the large international wage differentials with which we are concerned evidently reflect enormous differences in the productivity of labour and not just differences in the degree of monopoly. If low-income, low-productivity peasants from underdeveloped countries migrate to high-wage, high-productivity employment in the urban centres of Western Europe and North America, world output and efficiency rise, not fall.

IV. CONCLUSIONS

International migrations have their origin in political as well as economic phenomena. Large numbers of people have been displaced by war, e.g. during Mozambique's long struggle for independence. Others have been forced to flee their country because of the violence exercised by the state against its own citizens, e.g. Chile. Still others have been expelled from their country of birth because they belonged to particular social classes or ethnic groups, e.g. in Uganda. These are relatively 'pure' cases of mass emigration arising as a consequence of political events.

In each of these cases, however, fundamental economic conflicts underlay and reinforced the political pressures which on the surface were responsible for migration. In other instances, economic phenomena were more prominent, as in the use of head taxes to force self-provisioning peasants to enter labour markets in which their bargaining power was weak. Fiscal policy, systems of forced labour and slavery have all been important historically in compelling rural folk to move from one location or activity to another—and to change their social and economic status.

The migrations with which we have been concerned in this chapter differ from the above in that the decision to emigrate is taken, without compulsion, by the individual migrant, or collectively by his family, largely on the basis of material self-interest. Such migrations are a symptom of disequilibria in the labour market and these disequilibria take the form of substantial differences in the expected income of working people in different regions or countries. The income differentials, in turn, arise from the low productivity of labour and the high degree of inequality in the underdeveloped countries as compared with the nations of Europe and North America.

Even the most superficial examination of the facts is sufficient to indicate that the pursuit of self-interest by peasant migrants is not incompatible with the rapid growth of *per capita* income in the country of emigration.[26] Indeed, in the countries of south and south-eastern Europe where emigration has been massive (Greece, Italy, Portugal, Spain and Yugoslavia), exceptionally rapid rates of growth have been achieved. Between 1960 and 1970 the growth of GNP *per capita* in the above five countries varied from 4.3 per cent a year in Yugoslavia to 6.6 per cent in Greece. Similar rates of growth of income per head have been achieved in recent years, i.e. 1968–73, in most of the underdeveloped countries of the Mediterranean basin from which emigration has been substantial: Turkey (4.5 per cent), Algeria (4.3 per cent during 1968–72) and Tunisia (6.5 per cent). Only Morocco, with a growth of income per head during this period of 0.8 per cent a year, failed to expand rapidly, and it would be a brave person indeed who would attribute Morocco's problems to emigration.

Conversely, the restrictions on immigration currently being adopted in almost all of the industrialised nations are likely to harm the prospects of several underdeveloped countries and to restrict severely the opportunities for betterment of the poorest people in these countries. That is, the burden of adjustment to reduced emigration will fall disproportionately on the lowest-income groups. In some regions, notably the Caribbean, the effects may be calamitous. Inequality already is increasing; unemployment is high and rising, and of those under 25 years of age, perhaps more than 50 per cent have no job; in the least developed countries of the region, the savings rate is negative and investment depends entirely on outside capital. In these circumstances, a reduction in opportunities to obtain employment abroad and the subsequent decline in remittances are likely to cause severe and prolonged transitional difficulties.

In summary, the disadvantages of mass emigration are unclear and almost certainly exaggerated, while the advantages are obvious. The migrants and those who receive remittances benefit directly. Other members of the migrants' social class benefit indirectly from less competition for jobs and increased bargaining strength. As a result, the emigration of the peasantry leads to an improvement in the distribution of income at the expense of those who rely for a livelihood on income from property. There is no evidence that emigration reduces a country's rate of growth, and in principle it could raise it. Thus, those who are concerned with achieving social justice for the working people of underdeveloped countries should condemn the restrictive immigration policies of rich countries and desist from encouraging poor countries to believe that it may be in their own interest to discourage emigration.

ADDENDUM

The question arises as to whether our conclusions about the benefits of international migration can be generalised to include rural–urban migration within a single country. At first glance it might appear that it makes little difference, say, whether an Anatolian peasant migrates to Istanbul or to Stuttgart. On the other hand, much recent literature, strongly influenced by the pioneering work of Michael Todaro,[27] suggests that internal migration entails a social cost in the form of reduced output in rural areas and increased unemployment in urban areas.

Personally, I doubt that this is an accurate description of the effects of migration. I readily concede, however, that the net benefits of internal migration are likely to be less than the benefits of international migration, partly because differentials in expected income will be narrower for internal migration and partly because any external diseconomies generated by migration—such as urban congestion—will be inflicted on compatriots rather than on foreigners. These differences clearly affect orders of magnitude, but it is unlikely that the general conclusions of our previous analysis need be altered.

The strong presumption remains that the private benefits of migration are positive. In fact, there is a growing body of quantitative evidence that indicates (i) that migration results in higher incomes for the migrants, (ii) that labour-force participation rates among migrants are higher than the average for urban areas, and (iii) that the unemployment rate of migrants in the cities is lower than the unemployment rate among the urban-born. Evidently the migrant is not confronted with the harsh alternative of either finding a job in the small 'formal sector' with its high but institutionally fixed wages, or becoming unemployed. Entry into the large flexible income sector—the 'informal sector'—is easy, and the majority of migrants readily obtain a livelihood there.

Internal migration is likely to improve the distribution of income in rural areas, for reasons already discussed, and accelerate capital formation and technical change on small peasant farms. Migration, in effect, enables the peasantry to overcome the imperfections of the rural credit market by creating opportunities to amass finance capital in the cities for subsequent investment in agriculture.[28] Migration to the cities, and the resulting greater access to educational facilities, also is a way for some members of the peasantry to accumulate 'human capital'. In the absence of improvements in the rural credit market and in the provision of education in rural areas, migration may be a second-best optimum.

Unfortunately, the reduction in income inequality in the countryside is likely to be accompanied by an increase in inequality in the cities. This is because massive rural – urban migration will tend to depress real incomes in the 'informal sector' and thereby accentuate differences between earned incomes in the fixed and flexible wage sectors, and possibly also increase the share in total urban income of income from property. Provided the migrants come from the lowest-income groups in the rural areas, however, the overall distribution of income is bound to improve, regardless of what statistical measure of inequality is used.

None of the foregoing should be construed as a defence of the system which induces the peasantry to migrate. Our claim is merely that migration is a second-best optimum. The first-best policies in many countries would include a redistribution of land (which would raise peasant incomes and, if correctly managed, increase total agricultural output as well), an improvement in the terms of trade of the agricultural sector (by reducing tariffs on industrial products), greater provision of public services in rural areas (especially education, health and electric power), and a reform of the rural credit market.

Attempts to reduce internal migration directly, for example by issuing internal passports, introducing border taxes at provincial boundaries or instructing the police to evict migrants from urban shanties, will aggravate the poverty problem, increase the cost of doing business in the 'informal sector', and thereby reduce the output of goods and services originating there and, ironically, probably reduce agricultural production as well. Neither equity nor efficiency is achieved by being nasty to migrant peasants.

NOTES AND REFERENCES

1. See, for example, Ch. 1.
2. ILO, *Time for Transition* (Geneva, 1975), p. 65.

3. W. R. Böhning, 'Some thoughts on emigration from the Mediterranean basin', *International Labour Review* (Geneva), Vol. 111, no. 3, pp. 251–77.
4. W. R. Böhning, 'Mediterranean workers in Western Europe: effects on home countries and countries of employment', International Labour Office, World Employment Programme, Working Paper (July 1975).
5. Suzanne Paine, *Exporting Workers: The Turkish Case* (University of Cambridge, Department of Applied Economics, Occasional Paper 41; University of Cambridge Press, 1974), Table 8, p. 89 and Table 12b, p. 187. Ms Paine has compiled a large amount of empirical information on emigration from Turkey and concluded that the net benefits from migration have been slight and perhaps even negative. Her own data, however, can be used to cast doubt on her conclusions.
6. By 'peasant' we mean any person who tills the soil either as a labourer or small proprietor. Many sociologists confine the term to the latter category, but at this stage of our analysis we do not wish to differentiate among the rural working population.
7. A. K. Sen, 'Peasants and dualism with or without surplus labour', *Journal of Political Economy*, Vol. 74 (1966).
8. Throughout most of this chapter it is assumed that the cost of migration is neglible in comparison with the wage received abroad and can be ignored.
9. The proviso might not hold if the migrant were ignorant of conditions in the receiving country. In such circumstances, however, one would expect reverse migration to occur or, at least, the cessation of emigration as would-be migrants learn of the experience of their predecessors.
10. It must be recognised, however, that emigration of the head of the household causes disruption to the family and this constitutes a social cost. In some cases families have been abandoned by migrants, and, where the wage income of the migrant constitutes the sole means of support of the women and children, considerable hardship may be inflicted upon them. On the other hand, if the migrant owns land, the remaining members of the household may be able to maintain and even improve their standard of living by renting out the land.
11. This may not be possible, however, if the household consists of near-subsistence farmers with inadequate cash income and severe marketing difficulties.
12. W. R. Böhning, 'Some thoughts on emigration from the Mediterranean basin', loc. cit., p. 260; emphasis in the original.
13. We disregard the likelihood of diminishing returns to labour and for the sake of simplicity assume the line to be straight.
14. Several externalities, which could introduce a divergence between private and social benefit, are mentioned below.
15. ILO, op. cit.
16. Suzanne Paine, op. cit., Table 10, p. 102.
17. See Ch. 3.
18. This will occur, in Figure 7, provided only that the household adopts a position on G_3t' that is not to the right of E_4, since at E_4 total consumption is just equal to the amount produced before emigration OQ plus current remittances OR. Note that this condition for the maintenance of production is consistent with a substantial increase in leisure.

19. W. R. Böhning, 'Mediterranean workers in Western Europe', loc. cit., p. 24.
20. Suzanne Paine, op. cit., Table A17, p. 192.
21. Ibid., Table A19, p. 194. It is difficult to reconcile these facts with Ms Paine's conclusion that Turkish migrants 'have come mainly from the middle and upper middle ranks of the peasantry . . .' (ibid., p. 123).
22. In fact the correct figure is closer to six times higher. See ibid., Table 10, p. 102.
23. Since the productivity of labour is higher in urban areas than in rural, emigration results in a rise in GDP per head of the remaining population.
24. W. R. Böhning, 'Mediterranean workers in Western Europe', loc. cit., p. 25.
25. See the quotation from *Time for Transition* on the first page of this chapter.
26. It is possible that migration affects population growth, e.g., if the migrants are young, unmarried men, the change in age composition in the country of emigration will reduce population growth.
27. M. P. Todaro, 'A model of labour migration and urban unemployment in less developed countries', *American Economic Review* (Mar. 1969).
28. I am grateful to Oded Stark for calling my attention to this point.

5. The new international economic order

The spokesmen for the heterogeneous group of countries known as the Third World have long expressed dissatisfaction with the existing institutional arrangements and policies which govern international economic intercourse. Dissatisfaction, however, has increased in recent years and has become highly vociferous, at times even acrimonious. This change in mood is due to a series of factors: the increase in the number of newly independent poor countries and their emergence as an organised majority in several international institutions, notably in the General Assembly of the United Nations; the success of the Organization of Petroleum Exporting Countries (OPEC) in raising prices and thereby substantially increasing their real income, largely at the expense of the rich industrial countries; the decline in the political power and influence of the West, particularly after the defeat of the United States in Vietnam; and the combination of depressed production and rapidly rising prices which has characterised the world economy for most of the present decade.

The Third World, no longer content merely to criticise present arrangements, have put forward a set of proposals designed to create a New International Economic Order (NIEO). These proposals were embodied in a resolution of a Special Session of the UN General Assembly in the spring of 1974 and are therefore official policy of the United Nations Organization. Before turning to an examination of the NIEO let us briefly review the origins, objectives and results of the present order which it is intended to replace.

I. THE PRESENT ORDER

The present international economic system is essentially a product of the 1940s and represents an attempt by the dominant powers of the time, pre-eminently the United States, to recreate an integrated world economy out of the disarray that prevailed for a decade and a half between the financial collapse on Wall Street in 1929 and the destruction of Nagasaki by the second atomic bomb in 1945. There were three major objectives that the architects of the present system hoped to achieve.

First, they wanted to establish a world monetary and trading system conducive to a relatively free flow of commodities and private capital. Accordingly the International Monetary Fund (IMF) was launched at Bretton Woods in 1944 and charged with responsibility for maintaining order in foreign exchange markets and providing short-term loans to help member countries overcome balance of payments difficulties. The General Agreement on Tariffs and Trade (GATT) was charged with promoting freer trade by generally proscribing import quotas and encouraging the reduction in tariffs through a series of bargaining rounds, the first of which was held in Geneva in 1947.

The second objective was to facilitate the post-war reconstruction of Europe and contribute to the finance of development in the under-developed countries, many of them newly independent ex-colonial countries. One way this was done was by creating an International Bank for Reconstruction and Development (IBRD), at the same time and place as the IMF, to provide long-term loans on favourable conditions to finance agreed projects. Another way was through America's Greek-Turkish aid programme of 1947 and the 1948–52 European Recovery Programme, supported by the Marshall Plan, the forerunners of the bilateral aid programmes.

The third objective was to create harmonious economic relations and, when this became impossible, machinery for resolving disputes through negotiation rather than violence. A seemingly endless number of specialised agencies were established under the United Nations umbrella to deal with technical issues concerning food and agriculture (FAO), education (UNESCO), health (WHO), etc. Legal conflicts were to be handled by the International Court of Justice in The Hague, which in 1946 rose like a phoenix from the ashes of the Permanent Court of International Justice established by the old League of Nations. Finally, political disputes were to be resolved by an institution created at a conference in San Francisco in 1945, the United Nations itself, and particularly by the UN Security Council on which the victors of the Second World War (USA, USSR, Britain, France and China) had permanent seats and a veto.

The ideology of this post-war system is capitalist: free enterprise, freer trade, relatively free movement of currencies across the exchanges (occasionally, as now, even some freely-floating exchange rates). The ideology, however, has been implemented in a pragmatic rather than dogmatic way. Free enterprise has been tempered by state planning (particularly in the underdeveloped countries); free trade has been modified by tariff protection (particularly in the underdeveloped countries) and by non-tariff barriers to trade (particularly in the developed ones); currency movements have been restricted by capital controls. Despite these qualifications, it is clear that the underlying purpose in establishing the economic order was to allow the logic of the market to determine the pattern of production, the location of economic activity and the distribution of income on a worldwide scale. Considerations of equity were subservient to those of efficiency.

The ideology of the economic order was American; so too was much of the money that financed the institutions responsible for maintaining that order. The United Nations, for example, began with a $65 million interest-free loan from the United States and gifts of $8.5 million and $2 million, respectively, from John D. Rockefeller, Jr and New York City. For many years, indeed until the present order began to crumble, the US contribution accounted for 39 per cent of the regular budget of the United Nations, or three-and-a-half times more than the next-largest contributor. (By 1971 the US contribution had fallen to 31.5 per cent.) A similar situation existed, and largely continues to exist, in the IMF and IBRD. The original quota of the United States in the Fund was 31 per cent of the total, fractionally larger than the quotas of the next four largest countries combined, and under the complicated voting system of the Fund, enough to give the US 27.93 per cent of total voting power and a veto on decisions and policy. In the Bank, too, voting is *pro rata* with the size of quota and the dominance of the US has been further ensured by the fact that the President of the Bank has always been an American.

The present order has been maintained not only with US money plus weighted voting but also by the use of force and the threat of military intervention. The Stockholm International Peace Research Institute (SIPRI) estimates that 'between 1957 and 1976, the world spent about $5,500,000 million, in constant 1976 dollars, on the military.'[1] If this cumulative expenditure is divided by the present population of the world, it is equivalent to about $1,300 for every man, woman and child alive. In 1976 alone, SIPRI estimates that total world military expenditure was between $334,000 million and more than $400,000 million.[2] This is more than the GNP of the entire African continent; it is more than the GNP of South America; in fact, it is more than the GNP of Africa and South America combined!

Clearly, world resources have been wasted on armaments on a massive scale and this obviously has reduced the level of household consumption and its rate of growth below what they otherwise might have been. Even so, the growth of the world economy, including the capitalist economies with which we are primarily concerned, has been rapid. If one measures the success of the present order by the rate of growth of output in the capitalist world, rich and poor countries alike, the present system undoubtedly has been successful. For example, between 1960 and 1973 gross domestic product in the rich and poor capitalist countries combined increased over five per cent a year, slightly faster than in the centrally planned economies.

This growth, however, occurred in a context of great inequality in the distribution of the world's income. Considering the globe as a whole, the poorest 71 per cent of the world's population in 1970 received only about 15 per cent of the world's GNP. Within the capitalist or market economy countries the poorest 72 per cent of the population received only 14 per cent of the income (see Table 9). The distribution of income within the world as a whole is as unequal as the distribution within any single country.

TABLE 9. Percentage distribution of world population and GNP, 1970

| | Percentage of world | | Percentage of market economy | |
	Population	GNP	Population	GNP
Market economy countries				
Developed	19	66	28	86
Underdeveloped	49	11	72	14
Centrally planned economies				
Developed	10	19	–	–
Underdeveloped	22	4	–	–
TOTAL	100	100	100	100

Source: Angelos Angelopoulos, *The Third World and the Rich Countries: Prospects for the Year 2000* (New York: Praeger, 1972) Table 3, p. 23.

Moreover, differences in average income between the rich and poor countries have been increasing. It is virtually inevitable, of course, that the absolute difference in income would increase given the initial disparities. That is, even if the rich and poor countries were growing at the same annual compound rate, the yearly increment in the income of the rich would exceed that of the poor because of the higher base to which the growth rate of the rich applies. Unfortunately, reality is even worse than this: it appears that the average incomes in rich countries are growing noticeably faster than in the poor. For instance, between 1960 and 1973, the rate of growth of GDP *per capita* in the capitalist underdeveloped countries was about 3.3 per cent a year, whereas in the advanced capitalist economies it was about 3.7 per cent a year.[3]

The impression given by these tendencies is supported by correlation analysis. Data were obtained for 107 capitalist countries, rich and poor, and the rank correlation was estimated between *per capita* GNP in 1960, measured in 1973 market prices, and the rate of growth of GNP *per capita* during 1960–73. The coefficient of rank correlation was 0.52. This indicates that countries which were relatively rich in 1960 tended to grow relatively rapidly during the following 13 years, while countries which were relatively poor tended to grow relatively slowly. This analysis provides some supporting evidence in favour of the proposition that inherent within a market economy system are forces which tend to maintain and even accentuate inequality in the distribution of income and wealth.[4]

The same tendency toward growing inequality is apparent within the Third World. From the set of 107 capitalist countries, 82 were identified as underdeveloped, namely those with a GNP per head in 1960 of less than $800 measured in 1973 prices. The coefficient of rank correlation was estimated as before and it turned out to be 0.46, slightly lower than in the previous case but still positive.[5] Again, this evidence is consistent with other available information. The IBRD, for example, has grouped the countries of the Third World into four categories: oil-producing, higher-income countries, middle-income and lower-income countries. The rate of growth of GDP *per capita* during 1960–73 of the four groups was, respectively, 4.9 per cent a year, 3.9, 3.2 and 1.2.[6] Growth rates declined systematically as one moved from high- to low-income countries.

Thus there can be little doubt that international inequality has increased since the present international economic order was established. It is this tendency of the system to produce greater inequality, and indeed to be compatible in many instances with the absolute impoverishment of sizeable groups of people,[7] that almost certainly accounts for the growing demands for a New International Economic Order.

These demands are directed against a system which is characterised not only by massive expenditure on armaments, as we have seen, but also by chronic violence, particularly in the Third World. SIPRI estimates that about 47 per cent of military expenditure is incurred by the United States and its North Atlantic Treaty Organization (NATO) allies, 23 per cent by the USSR and its Warsaw Treaty Organization (WTO) allies, and only 7 per cent by the Third World.[8] Within the Third World 73 per cent of the military spending is accounted for by 10 countries, the others having relatively small military budgets.

Most weapons are designed and produced in the NATO and WTO countries, 70 per cent of the world's military spending occurs in these countries, yet 'about three-quarters of the current global arms trade is with Third World countries.'[9] Moreover, it is in the poor countries that the violent confrontations usually occur. In the three decades since the present international order was established there have been a total of 119 civil and international wars. These wars have involved the military forces of 81 countries and the territory of 69 countries, mostly in the Third World. The present international order, including its economic arrangements, thus stands condemned in the eyes of many, not because it has been unable to produce rapid global growth, which it has, but because it has perpetuated inequality and violence on a mammoth scale.

II. THE INTERNATIONAL TRADING SYSTEM

The core of the present order is the trade and payments system. From the point of view of the developed market economy countries this system has performed fairly well: world trade has expanded rapidly, in fact faster than world output, and despite occasional measures to protect domestic production, on the whole there has been considerable liberalisation of trade among the industrial countries. The under-developed countries view the situation rather differently, however.

First, they have not participated fully in the expansion of world trade. As Singer and Ansari report, 'the share of the developing countries in total world exports fell from 31.2 per cent in 1950 to 17.4 per cent in 1972, whereas the share of the Western developed countries rose from 60 per cent to 72.3 per cent over the same period.'[10]

Second, the underdeveloped countries are dissatisfied with the commodity composition of their trade and in particular with the continued heavy reliance on exports of primary commodities. It is true that exports of manufactured goods from the underdeveloped countries grew rapidly in the decade of the 1960s, viz. about 14 per cent a year, and as a result the share of manufactured goods in their total exports rose from 7 per cent in 1953 to about a quarter today. But this trade is concentrated on a few products, notably clothing and textiles, and in a relatively few countries. The great majority of Third World countries must still rely on exports of minerals and agricultural products.

Third, to add injury to insult, the share of primary commodity trade in world trade is falling and the share of the underdeveloped countries in primary commodity trade is also tending to fall. Of course what is true of the average is not necessarily true of all the commodities which comprise the average, and the export prospects of some primary commodities are very bright, e.g. petroleum. Moreover, the tendency for the underdeveloped countries to experience a declining share even in primary commodity trade may be due in some cases to limitations of supply rather than to inadequate demand.

There is no doubt, however, that restricted demand is part of the problem. In particular, fourth, protectionism in the rich countries discriminates heavily against imports from poor countries. Effective tariff protection of agricultural production in the rich countries is high and rising. This has severely damaged the export possibilities of some primary products, e.g. sugar, fruit, meat, fats and oils. Moreover, tariff protection is supplemented by numerous non-tariff barriers to trade which hit the underdeveloped countries disproportionately hard. These non-tariff barriers include such things as cumbersome administrative regulations, safety rules, health standards, government procurement policies and a few outright quotas. Exports of manufactured goods from the Third World also are discriminated against. 'The structure of tariffs in the industrial nations in the mid-1970s discriminates powerfully against the processing of raw materials in developing countries.'[11] Indeed one study indicates that the effective tariffs in rich countries on imports of manufactured goods from poor countries were twice as high in 1972 as the average effective tariff on rich countries' imports of manufactures from 'all countries', viz. 22.6 per cent as compared to 11.1 per cent.[12] Moreover, actual protection and protectionist sentiment in the rich countries are increasing.

Fifth, despite numerous attempts by groups of Third World countries to encourage trade amongst themselves, the dependency of the underdeveloped countries on export markets in the developed market economy countries not only is very high (about 74 per cent) but also rising. The proportion of exports from underdeveloped countries to other underdeveloped countries is falling, while that with the centrally planned economies is remaining roughly constant since the early 1960s at 5 to 6 per cent.[13] The dependency of the Third World countries on the West is not limited to export markets; they are dependent on the West also for much of their technology, foreign aid and loans and for their private foreign investment.

Finally, the Third World is concerned about the prices which their exports fetch in world markets, which in practice means the markets of the rich countries. The question of the long-term trend in the terms of trade is a highly vexed one, many spokesmen for the Third World contending that the terms of trade are moving against the poor countries and against primary commodities. The two are not the same, of course: many rich countries export primary commodities, e.g. Australia and the USA, and some poor countries export manufactured goods, e.g. Taiwan.

The facts of the matter are ambiguous. Long-term trends are impossible to estimate accurately because of inadequate data, the changing composition of trade and improvements in the quality of goods traded over time. Medium-term trends are difficult to calculate because of the sensitivity of estimates to the choice of base year. If one takes 1960 as the base year, however, it appears that the terms of trade of the underdeveloped countries remained constant for a decade, then improved noticeably until 1973 and dramatically in 1974–6. The oil-producing countries obviously were major beneficiaries of the change in relative prices, but the higher-income underdeveloped countries also experienced gains. The poorest of the underdeveloped countries, in contrast, suffered a deterioration.[14]

If one looks at commodities rather than countries one finds that in the period since 1963 there may have been a slight tendency for the price index of primary products exported by the underdeveloped countries to rise less rapidly than the prices of primary products exported by the rich countries, but if there *was* such a tendency it was reversed in 1974 after the rise in oil prices. What is true of primary products as a whole is equally true of food prices, agricultural non-food prices and the export price of minerals; in the case of non-ferrous base metals, the price index for the underdevelped countries appears to have risen more rapidly throughout the period 1963–74 than the price index for the rich countries.[15]

Thus the debate over the commodity terms of trade is inconclusive. More serious is the fact that even if there were a clear tendency for the commodity terms of trade to move in one direction or the other, the welfare significance of this would be far from obvious. Suppose, for example, that the price of a country's export commodity Px fell relative to the price of its imports Pm, so that its commodity terms of trade Px/Pm deteriorated. The fall in the country's term of trade, however, would not necessarily signify a decline in its welfare, or its gains from trade, if the fall in prices were less than the fall in costs of production. That is, an increase in the productivity of the factors of production in the underdeveloped country's export sector πu might more than offset the fall in export prices. If this were to happen the so-called single factoral terms of trade $(Px/Pm)\pi u$ would improve and the country would enjoy an absolute increase in the benefits from trade.

On the other hand, if one is interested primarily in the relative distribution of the gains from trade between the underdeveloped and developed countries, rather than in whether the poor countries benefit absolutely, the relevant concept of the terms of trade is the so-called double factoral terms of trade. This corrects the commodity terms of trade by taking into account the productivity of the factors of production, not only in the export sector of the underdeveloped countries but in the export sector of the developed countries πd as well.[16] That is, the double factoral terms of trade for the underdevelped countries is defined as

$$Tdf \equiv \frac{Px}{Pm} \cdot \frac{\pi u}{\pi d}$$

It is evident from the above definition that the commodity terms of trade and the single factoral terms of trade of the underdeveloped countries could be improving while the double factoral terms of trade were deteriorating. If this were to happen it would imply that the underdeveloped countries received an absolute gain from trade but that the relative gains were distributed in favour of the rich countries. That is, the pattern of trade would be such that international inequality would tend to increase over time.

It was argued in Chapter 1 that, largely because of economies of scale and the faster pace of technical change in the rich countries, the double factoral terms of trade would tend to move against the poor countries and most of the benefits of trade would consequently accrue to the former. Until recently there was no empirical evidence with which to test this proposition, but a pioneering study for the United Nations Conference on Trade and Development (UNCTAD) by John Spraos has now provided some support.

Spraos attempted to measure the double factoral terms of trade not of underdeveloped countries but of primary commodities of underdeveloped countries *vis-à-vis* manufactured exports of developed ones. Specifically, his study included metals and six crops (cocoa, coffee, cotton, rubber, sugar and tea). His results indicate that over the decade 1960–70 the double factoral terms of trade of metals increased by about

13 per cent, while the double factoral terms of trade of the six crops decreased by about 28 per cent and of crops and metals combined by 14 to 20 per cent depending on the weighting system used.[17] Spraos concludes from his research 'that developing countries are trapped by the specialisation they inherited in a situation in which they cannot now improve their relative position by doing better what they have always done since colonial days.'[18]

This system of international trade favouring the rich countries is reinforced by a payments system which also favours them. The main reason for this is that most of the growth in reserves has been earmarked 'for the financing of the richest and most capitalised countries, irrespective of their policies, rather than for the financing of internationally agreed objectives, such as—among others—economic development of the poorest and most undercapitalised countries.'[19] This is a virtually inescapable consequence of the present payments system in which international reserves consist largely of the national currencies of the major Western trading countries and an increase in reserves is generated by the reserve currency countries, notably the USA, running a balance of payments deficit. Of the massive growth of world reserves over the five years 1970–5, a growth which is responsible in large part for financing the great inflation of the present decade, 'about 95 per cent was invested in the developed countries—mostly the United States—and only 3 per cent in the less developed countries. These reserve investments in the richest countries were about triple the total amount of recorded official assistance by the OECD countries to the developing countries.'[20]

The present payments system was supposed to have been reformed in January 1970 when the IMF issued the first Special Drawing Rights (SDRs). It was intended that SDRs would gradually become the principal reserve asset, replacing gold, the US dollar and other national currencies. After the first issue of $3,000 million SDRs they accounted for 4.3 per cent of total reserves. A year later an equal amount was issued and SDRs then accounted for 7.5 per cent of total reserves. Thereafter the proportion began to fall steadily and they are today of less significance than on the day after they were first issued. Gold and the dollar remain the most important reserve assets, and thus a modest reform, laboriously negotiated, has virtually vanished from sight. A more ambitious reform which would have favoured the Third World by linking the creation of SDRs with foreign aid has little chance of being implemented in the near future.

Instead, the focus of attention of the rich countries has been on the breakdown of the adjustable peg exchange rate regime negotiated at Bretton Woods in 1945. This regime lasted until 1971, when the authorities of many countries allowed the rate of exchange to float. Since then laissez-faire has prevailed as regards the exchange rate policy of the major trading countries and this new regime has been endorsed by the Jamaica Agreement of 1976. It is arguable that this transformation of the exchange rate regime is likely to have relatively little influence on growth rates in the Third World or elsewhere, since in the first instance changes in exchange rates affect primarily monetary variables rather than real ones, but there is little doubt that an international payments system could be devised, perhaps involving the creation by Third World countries of a new reserve asset of their own, which would improve the position of poor countries.[21]

III. THE NIEO AND THE 'INTEGRATED COMMODITY SCHEME'

The heart of the proposals to create a new international economic order is a reorganisation of trade in primary commodities. The Third World would like to diversify their exports, particularly into manufactured goods and away from those traditional primary commodities for which demand is growing slowly. Meanwhile, however, they have concentrated their demands on increasing the gains from the production and trade of raw materials and agricultural products. They have urged that prices of primary goods be stabilised, that downward trends in the commodity terms of trade be prevented, that international schemes be implemented on a large scale to compensate countries for falls in export earnings, that raw materials be processed in the country where they are produced, and that the underdeveloped countries obtain greater participation in the marketing and distribution of their exports.

Debate has focused on an 'integrated commodity scheme' designed by UNCTAD. The main feature of this scheme is provision for the stabilisation of the prices of 18 commodities (of which 10 are designated 'core' commodities) accounting for 80 per cent of total commodity trade excluding oil, through the creation of a $6 billion Common Fund.

Several points can be raised about this scheme. First, it is uncertain that export instability as such is generally very harmful to development, although it may be unpleasant and inconvenient.[22] Second, it is uncertain that stabilising prices will in fact stabilise incomes; if the source of instability is variations in supply rather than demand, stabilising prices will destabilise income. Third, assuming stabilisation of prices is on balance beneficial, it is uncertain that a scheme which merely stabilises prices will effect a redistribution of the world's income to primary product exporting countries (many of which are rich countries) let alone effect a significant redistribution from the developed to the underdeveloped countries. Fourth, assuming there is a redistribution in favour of the Third World, it is uncertain that many benefits will accrue to some of the very populous and very poor countries such as India where the ratio of primary commodity exports to national income is low. Finally, even if the benefits do reach the poorest countries, it is unclear that they will reach the poorest people in the poorest countries rather than be captured, for instance, by plantation owners, large landowners, ranchers and export merchants.

Thus the price stabilisation feature of the 'integrated commodity scheme' may merit neither the passionate advocacy it has received from the Third World nor the intense hostility it has received from the USA, Germany and other developed countries. The scheme contains other features, of course, but these are of relatively minor significance. For example, indexation of commodity prices may not be important if, as we have suggested earlier, there is in fact no discernible long-run tendency for the commodity terms of trade to deteriorate; the analogy between the indexation proposal and the price-support-cum-trade-protection policies used to protect the agricultural sector of Western countries may not be appropriate. Again, greater use of long-term bulk supply contracts is unlikely to result in faster growth in the Third World or a more equal distribution of world income. Provision already exists at the IMF for compensating countries for declines in export receipts; at present this facility is still rather limited, but it could be substantially expanded and liberalised by breaking the link between the amount a country can borrow and its quota at the Fund and by increasing the amount of compensation for any given shortfall of exports. Better still would be to compensate for any shortfall in the capacity to import regardless of whether this occurred as a result of lower export prices or quantities or higher import prices.

In summary, the 'integrated commodity scheme' is very modest. Even if it were implemented fully it is unlikely that it would have much of an impact on reducing international inequality, although it would do no harm. A reallocation of world resources which permitted labour-intensive processing industries to shift to the underdeveloped countries would undoubtedly be beneficial to rich and poor countries alike once the problems of adjustment had been overcome, but given the high unemployment rates in rich countries it is doubtful that such a reallocation would be allowed to occur. Stabilising commodity prices, introducing more 'orderly' markets through long-term purchase agreements and compensating countries for export fluctuations may also be desirable, but none of these measures will alter fundamentally a situation in which seven-tenths of the world's population receives little more than one-seventh of the world's income. In the few cases, notably tropical beverage products, where import demand elasticities are low, higher rather than more stable primary commodity prices are needed. Even better would be a direct transfer of resources to poor countries through grants and other forms of aid.

IV. DIMINISHING GENEROSITY OF THE RICH

The rich nations, led by the USA, have already voiced their hostility to arrangements which would lead to higher commodity prices. In particular, they have strongly opposed the formation of producer cartels of the OPEC type. Equally, the rich nations, again led by the USA, have by their actions expressed hostility to transferring resources to the Third World through larger aid programmes.

At the end of the last decade a 'grand assize' was organized by the IBRD in an attempt to revive the flagging enthusiasm for aid. The Report of the Commission on International Development, commonly known as the Pearson Report, contained a recommendation 'that each industrialised country increase its resource transfer to low-income countries to a minimum of 1 per cent of its GNP as rapidly as possible and in no case later than 1975.'[23] It was further recommended that 'official development assistance' (ODA), i.e. grants and soft loans, etc. by official agencies, become 0.7 per cent of GNP' by 1975 or shortly thereafter, but in no case later than 1980.'[24]

Since these recommendations were made, however, the situation has deteriorated rather than improved.[25] The net flow of resources, both private and official, was a higher proportion of the GNP of donor countries in 1965 than it was in 1975. As regards ODA, it fell from 0.53 per cent of the GNP of the industrialised countries in 1961 to 0.36 per cent in 1975 and then remained constant for the next two years. Over the period 1961–75 the real value of official development assistance increased only 0.7 per cent a year, far less than the population of the Third World, so that real aid per head in the underdeveloped countries fell sharply. During this same period the GNP of the rich countries increased in real terms by 80 per cent.

The United States is the largest donor of official development assistance, accounting for nearly 30 per cent of the total in the first half of the current decade. In terms of its GNP, however, the United States is one of the least generous of the rich countries. Five countries in 1974–5 gave more than one per cent of their GNP in the form of official development assistance; all of them were much maligned Arab oil-exporting countries, led by Qatar with 5.43 per cent of its GNP. The most generous industrialised countries were Sweden and the Netherlands, the first of which exceeded the 0.7 per cent target and the second achieved it exactly. The United States was in 20th position in the league table with only 0.25 per cent of its GNP devoted to aid, far behind less prosperous countries such as Belgium (0.55) or even the United Kingdom (0.38). Moreover, the United States was moving steadily away from the target, its aid having been 0.53 per cent of GNP in the early 1960s. Indeed, in real terms US aid declined by 5.6 per cent a year during 1960–75.[26]

Given the diminishing generosity of the largest contributor, the prospects for conventional aid programmes evidently are not bright. It is to be expected, therefore, that the Third World will increasingly seek relatively unorthodox ways of transferring resources from the rich countries. One proposal, long advocated and much discussed, would create additional international reserve assets in the form of SDRs and allocate them to underdeveloped countries.[27] This 'link' proposal, however, has never encountered favour in the industrialised countries and, as mentioned above, is unlikely to be implemented in the current period of abundant international reserves.

Rather than create additional assets, perhaps the foreign debt liabilities of the Third World could be reduced. The easiest way to do this would be to convert all or part of the official foreign debt owed to foreign countries into grants.[28] Another possibility would be to 'internationalise' world resources at present unexploited and not yet under firm national control, notably the seabed and the Antarctic, and to use any revenues or rents generated to raise the income of poor countries.

All of these proposals, and others that could be devised, are feasible and would result in a larger flow of resources to the Third World. The problem is not to invent a mechanism for transferring resources but to discover whether 'certain ways of financing the transfer of resources might be more acceptable to them (i.e. to the rich countries) than some others. It is only this possibility which provides the justification for the search for new mechanisms of transfer.'[29] The evidence does not suggest that the rich countries are inclined to be more generous to the poor. On the contrary, 'the problem is basically one of the absence of a strongly-felt need on the part of the rich countries.'[30] If this is so, it may be that the rhetoric of the present order—a rhetoric of foreign assistance, of partnership in development, of international co-operation—will give way to increased confrontation between those countries which control most of the world's resources and those which contain most of the population.

V. THIRD WORLD PARTICIPATION IN INTERNATIONAL AFFAIRS

When the United Nations was founded in 1945 there were only 51 members, few from Africa or Asia although 20 from Latin America; in 1977 there were 144 members, the great majority from the Third World. This change in the composition of the United Nations, however, has not been fully reflected in a corresponding increase in the influence of Third World countries in the major institutions of the international system. The United Nations Organization undoubtedly is undergoing change, but it remains essentially a plutocracy. There is still a long way to go before power is effectively based on one country, one vote; the distance from this to equal representation of all persons in the world, be they Englishmen or Indonesians, is much farther off still. This imbalance in political power between rich and poor countries is one of the features of the present order that the latter seek to overcome. Indeed the demand for a new international economic order is a demand for a redistribution of power—political and economic—as well as a demand for a re-distribution of income. The Common Fund for commodities is ul-timately less important than the common cause of the Third World as articulated by the Group of 77. That is, the NIEO should be viewed not as a single package of reforms but as a process in which the Third World gradually acquires greater economic and political power.

Voting in the IBRD is heavily weighted in favour of the rich countries. At present the Third World have about 38.5 per cent of the voting power as compared to 42.5 per cent held by the major industrial countries and another 19 per cent held by the other industrial countries. Spokesmen for the poor countries have become dissatisfied with their relatively small participation in determining Bank policy and have put forward a modest initial proposal that the votes be divided equally between the industrialised nations and the Third World.[31] Whatever the success of this proposal, it can be expected that the underdeveloped countries will continue to exert pressure to obtain greater influence within the Bank.

Similar pressure is being exerted within the IMF. At the moment the underdeveloped countries have 28 per cent of the total votes. A proposal to modify the existing weighted voting procedure is under active discussion, however. If this proposal were accepted the number of votes of the non-oil-exporting underdeveloped countries would remain unchanged, but the votes of the OPEC countries would double from 5 to 10 per cent of the total. Thus the votes of Third World countries would rise to 33 per cent, enough in principle to give them a veto over operational decisions of the Fund (which require a 70 per cent majority). At the same time the United States would retain its veto over decisions with a substantial political content (which require an 85 per cent majority).

Not only the financial agencies but also the specialised technical agencies of the UN are likely to experience rapid change as the poor exercise their collective power. Heretofore the specialised agencies, in the name of technical assistance, have acted as conveyor belts, transferring knowledge, institutions and practice from the Western nations to their former colonies and near-colonies in Asia, Africa and Latin America. The senior management of the agencies have come largely from the rich countries and it is the rich countries which have controlled the budgets and the policies of the agencies.

In one agency after another, however, constitutional and political crises have occurred. The International Labour Organisation (ILO) is a good example. The Governing Board of the ILO contains 56 seats; 28 of these are occupied by governments, of which 10 are reserved for so-called States of Chief Industrial Importance. Only one of these reserved seats belongs to an underdeveloped country (India); the rest are occupied by 8 rich capitalist countries and the USSR. This arrangement is no longer acceptable to the Third World and they have demanded that the constitution of the ILO be radically altered. The United States reacted to this demand, and to other provocative actions taken by members of the ILO, by notifying the Organisation in November 1975 of its intent to withdraw and by doing so exactly two years later.

Behind the constitutional crisis in the ILO are others of substance and form. The ILO, unique among UN agencies, is a tripartite institution with representatives of government, workers and management. The government view, as we have seen, is weighted in favour of the rich countries. The management view is weighted in favour of the large multinational corporations and the labour view is weighted in favour of those who are organised into formal trades unions. Nine-tenths of the workers in the underdeveloped countries, however, are unorganised. Indeed, most of those who labour in this world are peasants of one sort or another and apart from the unionised plantation workers very few workers in rural areas belong to a labour movement. Yet ever since it was established by the League of Nations in 1919 the ILO has been Western trade union oriented. The difficulty is that this orientation is no longer consonant with the needs of the majority of member countries, and it is this which lies at the roots of the ILO's crisis.

It is safe to predict that the conveyor belt of the conventional technical assistance programmes will decline in importance as the specialised agencies attempt to adjust to the demands placed upon them by their new constituents. It is more difficult to foresee the direction in which the agencies will evolve. It is likely, however, that hard bargaining between rich and poor countries will become increasingly important, replacing the donor – recipient and patron – client relationships, and some of the agencies may provide facilities where this bargaining can take place. UNCTAD already plays such a role for some issues.

If the Third World is to be successful in bargaining it will require much more information than is at present available. The UN agencies are well placed to lead the way in the collection, analysis and dissemination of information relevant to the establishment of a new international order. The proposed research programme of the recently-created Centre on Transnational Corporations may be indicative of the direction in which the UN will move. Before the other agencies can do so, however, they will require a major change in policy, reducing the emphasis on 'action', i.e. technical assistance and field projects, and purging 'research' of the pejorative connotation that now surrounds it. The UN must recognise that competent research is the best form of technical assistance.

The Third World cannot rely exclusively on the United Nations system to undertake the research and prepare the policy papers needed to negotiate a new international economic order. Just as the rich countries have their own collective institutions, e.g. the OECD and the Trilateral Commission, so too the poor countries must create institutions of their own to serve their interests. The time has come, surely, for the Group of 77 to establish a permanent secretariat and by so doing to demonstrate that the underdeveloped countries intend to participate actively and collectively in shaping future international affairs.

VI. CONCLUSIONS

We have argued that the present order was established largely by the rich countries, that they have been the major beneficiaries of the trade and payments system and that existing arrangements perpetuate and perhaps even accentuate international inequality. The specific proposals that have been put forward to create a new international economic order are very modest and any measures likely to be implemented are unlikely to result in a significant transfer of income to the Third World.

The political power of the poor countries has increased and they can be expected in the near future to acquire a dominant influence within the technical and financial agencies of the United Nations system. It is notable that in the International Fund for Agricultural Development, which became operational in 1977, the Third World countries have two-thirds of the votes. That is, the votes are equally shared among three categories of countries: recipient underdeveloped countries; donor Third World countries, i.e. OPEC countries; and developed donor countries.

Once the Third World obtains control of the United Nations it is likely that revised and more radical proposals to reorganise the international economy will be formulated. This, in turn, will lead to much harder bargaining between rich and poor countries than has so far occurred. The rich countries will remain in a powerful bargaining position, of course, but as the real aid ratio declines they will have less to offer and the underdeveloped countries will have correspondingly less to lose.

Furthermore, provided the Group of 77 can maintain its cohesiveness, the oil exporters and other newly prosperous countries avoiding the temptation to be co-opted into the club of rich countries and the rest of the group avoiding the tendency to concentrate on what divides rather than what unites them, the Third World too will be in a strong bargaining position.[32] It can try to follow OPEC's example and establish producer cartels for other primary commodities. It can follow the example of the Andean Group and try to impose tougher contractual terms on multinational corporations and impose tighter restrictions on the repatriation of income by multinationals. It can follow Taiwan's example and refuse to recognise copyright conventions; or go further and refuse to recognise patent and trade mark conventions. All of these measures would transfer income from rich to poor countries. It is also possible to increase the net assets of the Third World at the expense of rich countries. For instance, the Third World could follow the example of the southern states of the United States after the civil war and default on the foreign debt. There are numerous possibilities and no doubt some of them will be implemented.

Even if the distribution of income between rich and poor countries were to become more equal, however, it does not follow necessarily that the poorest people in the poorest countries would benefit. Indeed the question arises whether the new international economic order, any new international order, could by itself make a significant contribution to increasing the well-being of those who live in poverty. After all, the same economic forces that operate at the world level also operate inside the economies of most underdeveloped countries and the results are broadly similar, namely, a high degree of concentration of income and wealth. It is quite possible, therefore, that any resources that might be transferred to the Third World by a new order would immediately be appropriated by the relatively affluent within the underdeveloped countries.

This is not an argument against reforming the international economy. On the contrary, the case for doing so is clear. But if the international reforms are to have a favourable impact on poverty it seems equally clear that they must be complemented by reforms in the underdeveloped countries designed to ensure that the benefits of the system of production and distribution accrue primarily to those most in need.

National and international reforms are complementary but asymmetrical. National reforms in any Third World country can be devised which are certain to reduce poverty, as the experience of several countries indicates, but international reforms, in the absence of national ones, cannot be guaranteed to do so. It follows from this that if foreign military intervention can be avoided, no government need wait on a new international economic order before embarking on an anti-poverty programme, but if and when the dawn of a new order breaks the task of government should be somewhat easier.

NOTES AND REFERENCES

1. Frank Barnaby, 'Arms and the Third World: the Background', *Development Dialogue* (1977) 1, p. 21.
2. Ibid.
3. IBRD, *World Tables 1976* (Baltimore: Johns Hopkins University Press, 1976) Series III, Table 1, p. 392.
4. See Ch. 1.
5. The original data for the analysis were obtained from the *World Bank Atlas 1975*. The estimated coefficients of rank correlation were statistically highly significant.
6. IBRD, *World Tables 1976, loc. cit.* Lower-income countries were defined as those with a 1972 GNP *per capita* in 1972 US dollars of $200 or less; middle-income, $201–375; upper-income, above $375.
7. See Ch. 6.
8. Frank Barnaby, op. cit., Table 2, p. 23.

9. Ibid., p. 24. See also Anthony Sampson, *The Arms Bazaar* (London: Hodder and Stoughton, 1977).

10. Hans Singer and Javed Ansari, *Rich and Poor Countries* (London: Allen and Unwin, 1977) p. 30.

11. Alasdair I. MacBean and V. N. Balasubramanyam, *Meeting the Third World Challenge* (London: Macmillan for the Trade Policy Research Centre, 1976) p. 172.

12. B. Balassa, *The Structure of Protection in Industrial Countries* (IBRD Report No. EC-152) as quoted in Singer and Ansari, op. cit., p. 80. Also see Alexander Yeats, 'An Analysis of the Incidence of Specific Tariffs on Developing Country Exports', *Economic Inquiry* (Mar. 1976).

13. Trade between the Third World and the socialist countries grew rapidly from virtually a zero base in the early 1950s, but in recent years trade with the socialist countries has increased at approximately the same rate as trade with the advanced capitalist countries. For an analysis of economic relations between the socialist countries and the Third World see the special issue of *World Development* (May 1975) devoted to the subject.

14. See UNCTAD, *Review of International Trade and Development* (1975); IBRD, *World Tables 1976* (Baltimore: Johns Hopkins University Press, 1976) Series III, Table 11, p. 472.

15. See UN, *Monthly Bulletin of Statistics*, various issues.

16. For a discussion of the different concepts of the terms of trade see Jacob Viner, *Studies in the Theory of International Trade*, Ch. IX.

17. John Spraos, 'Is the Pattern of International Specialisation Fair to the Developing Countries?', mimeo., (Jan. 1976) Table 4 and 6.

18. Ibid., p. 15.

19. Robert Triffin, 'Jamaica: "Major Revision" or Fiasco?' in Edward M. Bernstein *et al.*, *Reflections On Jamaica*, Princeton Essays in International Finance, No. 115, (Apr. 1976) p. 46.

20. Ibid.

21. See, for example, Frances and Michael Stewart, 'Developing Countries, Trade and Liquidity: A New Approach', *The Banker* (Mar. 1972).

22. See Alasdair I. MacBean, *Export Instability and Economic Development* (London: Allen and Unwin, 1966). It can be argued, however, that it is in the interests of both rich and poor countries to stabilise commodity prices. See N. Kaldor, 'Inflation and Recession in the World Economy', *Economic Journal* (Dec. 1976). See also Karsten Laursen, 'The Integrated Programme for Commodities', *World Development* (Apr. 1978).

23. Lester B. Pearson, *Partners in Development* (London: Pall Mall Press, 1969) p. 147.

24. Ibid., p. 149.

25. See the annual publication of the OECD, *Development Cooperation: Efforts and Policies of the Members of the Development Assistance Committee.*

26. *Finance and Development* (June 1977) pp. 10—14.

27. This proposal has been advocated again most recently in a report to the Commonwealth Secretariat, *Towards a New International Economic Order* (London: HMSO, 1977).

28. This too was advocated in ibid., para. 8.54. Also see Nurul Islam, 'New Mechanisms for the Transfer of Resources to Developing Countries', UN

Journal of Development Planning (1977) pp. 84–92.
29. Nurul Islam, op. cit., p. 101.
30. Ibid.
31. Amon J. Nsekela, 'The World Bank and the New International Economic Order', *Development Dialogue* (1977) 1.
32. See C. Fred Bergsten, 'The Threat from the Third World', *Foreign Policy* (Summer 1973) and Paul Streeten, 'The Dynamics of the New Poor Power', *Resources Policy* (June 1976).

Part Two

National Poverty

6. Poverty in the Third World: ugly facts and fancy models*

Development of the type experienced by the majority of Third World countries in the last quarter century has meant, for very large numbers of people, increased impoverishment. This is the conclusion which has emerged from a series of empirical studies on trends in levels of living in the rural areas of Asia.[1] In most of the countries we have studied, the incomes of the very poor have been falling absolutely or the proportion of the rural population living below a designated 'poverty line' has been increasing, or both. Similar things almost certainly have been happening elsewhere, in Africa and parts of Latin America, for the mechanisms which generate growing poverty in Asia are present in greater or lesser degree in much of the rest of the underdeveloped world. Certainly there is no evidence that growth as such has succeeded in reducing the incidence of poverty.

I. PRINCIPAL FINDINGS

Ten empirical studies were undertaken in an attempt to determine the trends in the absolute and relative incomes of the rural poor in seven Asian countries. These seven countries were Bangladesh, India, Indonesia, Malaysia, Pakistan, Philippines and Sri Lanka. In the case of India it was thought that it would be meaningless to attempt to generalise about the entire country; instead, separate studies were made of conditions in four major states, viz. the Punjab, Uttar Pradesh, Bihar and Tamil Nadu.

The seven countries included in our sample account for approximately 70 per cent of the rural population of the non-socialist underdeveloped world. Since the average income of these seven countries is below that of the rest of the underdeveloped market

121

economy countries, it is likely that their share of the poor of the non-socialist underdeveloped world is even greater.

In each of the seven countries the scope and method of analysis had to be adapted to the available statistical information. Considerable differences in the quantity and quality of evidence were therefore inevitable. And yet some broad generalisations about trends are possible.

In general an attempt was made to cover as long a time period as possible and to bring the story forward as close to the present as possible. Attempts were made to overcome distortions due to weather cycles and to incorporate the most up-to-date information. But here too it was not possible to ensure uniformity. The period covered varies from a decade to a quarter century. The most outstanding facts to be noted are the worsening distribution of income and the declining real income of the rural poor. Those studies which contain the relevant data show that the shares of the lower decile groups in aggregate income and consumption have been declining even during periods of relatively rapid agricultural growth. There are significant differences from country to country as regards the proportion of its population that has been adversely affected, but in each country for which we have data, a substantial proportion of the lowest income groups appears to have experienced a decline in their share of real income over time.

Indeed, the evidence from the case studies points to an even stronger conclusion. In almost every case a significant proportion of low-income households experienced an absolute decline in their real income, particularly since the early 1960s.

This fact emerged from two separate types of measurements that were attempted in the case studies. First, a level of real income was defined below which all households were classified as poor. In most studies such a 'poverty line' was derived from an estimate of the level of income necessary to ensure a minimum diet, although the case studies differ widely as to what should be the contents of a minimum diet. In each case, however, it is found that the proportion of the population below the 'poverty line' either has remained constant or has tended in recent years to increase. The data are summarised in Table 10.

In six of the eight cases in which 'poverty lines' were constructed the proportion of the rural population in poverty seems to have increased, although in the Philippines the increase was modest. In Pakistan and Tamil Nadu, in contrast, the proportion of people in poverty has remained roughly constant.

One of the unsatisfactory things about 'poverty lines' is that it is

TABLE 10. Percentage of the rural population below the poverty line

Country or state	Year	Rural population in poverty		
		A	B	C
Pakistan	1963–4	72	54	45
	1966–7	64	52	44
	1968–9	64	53	46
	1969–70	68	46	36
	1970–1	71	47	38
	1971–2	74	55	43
Punjab, India	1960–1	18		
	1970–1	23		
Uttar Pradesh, India	1960–1	42		
	1970–1	64		
Bihar, India	1960–1	41		
	1963–4	54		
	1964–5	53		
	1970–1	59		
		A	B	
Tamil Nadu, India	1957–8	74	53	
	1959–60	79	54	
	1960–1	70	48	
	1961–2	66	36	
	1963–4	64	39	
	1964–5	72	46	
	1969–70	74	49	
		A	B	
Bangladesh	1963–4	40	5	
	1968–9	76	25	
	1973–4	79	42	
	1975	62	41	
Malaysia	1957	40		
	1970	47		
Philippines	1956–7	10		
	1961	12		
	1965	13		
	1970–1	12		

Source: The data were obtained from various chapters in Keith Griffin and Azizur Rahman Khan, eds., *op. cit.*, or, in the case of Malaysia and the Philippines, were derived from interpolations of data contained in that volume.

Notes:

(1) The data refer to the proportion of the rural population in poverty, except in the case of Malaysia and the Philippines, where the data refer to households.

(2) The poverty lines are defined as follows:

Pakistan: Income sufficient to yield food consumption satisfying 95% of the estimated caloric requirements (estimate *A*), or 92% (estimate *B*) or 90% (estimate *C*); *Punjab*: Rs. 16.36 *per capita* per month in 1960–1 prices; *Uttar Pradesh*: Rs. 14.50 *per capita* per month in 1960–1 prices; *Bihar*: Rs. 15.83 *per capita* per month in 1960–1 prices; *Tamil Nadu*: Rs. 21 *per capita* per month in 1960–1 prices (estimate *A*) or Rs. 15 *per capita* per month (estimate *B*); *Bangladesh*: Tk. 23.61 *per capita* per month in 1963–4 prices, corresponding to a level of income sufficient to yield food consumption satisfying 90% of the estimated caloric requirements (estimate *A*) or Tk. 17.02, corresponding to an income satisfying 80% of caloric requirements (estimate *B*); *Malaysia*: 97.4 Malaysian dollars per household per month at 1965 prices; *Philippines*: 434 pesos per family per year at 1965 prices; the reader is warned that these interpolations are tentative.

impossible to tell from them what has happened to the distribution of income among those below the line. This problem can be overcome in part, however, by constructing more than one line, corresponding to alternative definitions of poverty. This was done in three of the studies. In the case of Pakistan there appears to be no systematic tendency for the proportional incidence of rural poverty to change regardless of which of three definitions of poverty is used. The implication of this is that the distribution of income within the poverty group has remained essentially unaltered. In Tamil Nadu there has been no tendency for poverty to decline when the 'poverty line' is drawn at Rs. 21 *per capita* per month in 1960–1 prices (estimate *A*), but when the line is lowered to Rs.15 (estimate *B*) the proportion in poverty clearly has declined. This implies that the distribution of income among those with Rs. 21 *per capita* per month or less improved over the period studied. In Bangladesh, on the other hand, the proportion of the rural population with an income below the 'poverty line' of Tk. 23.6 *per capita* per month in 1963–4 prices rose significantly (estimate *A*), but the proportion below Tk. 17.02 (estimate *B*) rose even more dramatically, thereby indicating that inequality even among the poor became worse between 1963 and 1975.

A second type of measurement was a calculation of the real incomes of decile or quintile groups at different points of time. Here it was found that the real incomes of the lowest decile or quintile groups have been declining over time. Once again, the range over which this has occurred differs from one country to another. In the Philippines, for example, the bottom 20 per cent experienced a decline in real income, whereas in Bangladesh over 80 per cent of the population experienced such a decline.

The other major empirical finding concerns the trend in real wages of agricultural labourers. In most of the countries for which measurements could be obtained either real wages remained constant or there was a significant downward trend. In a few cases the trend was ambiguous, although even in these cases there was always clear additional evidence that the living standards of agricultural workers had not improved. In the Indian state of Punjab, for example, a few measurements suggest there was some increase in real wages of agricultural labourers, but the results are very sensitive to the wage series selected, the nature of the cost of living index used to convert nominal wages into real wages and the choice of the base year. At the same time, it has been shown in our study that the proportion of agricultural labourers below the poverty line increased precisely during the period when real wages are claimed to have risen. If one is to believe both pieces of evidence, then there must have been a change in the occupational distribution of the wage-earners included in the average wage index. In fact, the composition of agricultural labourers does seem to have changed significantly as a result of the widespread adoption of capital-intensive farming techniques, especially by the labour-hiring, large farmers. The importance of skilled labour and of operators of mechanical equipment has increased considerably. The rise in demand for workers of this type, given the initial shortage of skills, undoubtedly led to a relatively rapid increase in their wages. On the other hand, the balance between the supply and demand for more traditional types of labour became increasingly unfavourable over time, and consequently their wages failed to rise.

All of the countries included in our sample are characterised by a highly unequal distribution of land ownership. Statistical information usually relates to the distribution of farm size, i.e. to the area farmed and not the area owned. It is generally known that the ownership distribution is less equal than the distribution of farm size. Of the seven countries studied, the degree of inequality is perhaps the least in Bangladesh, but even there the bottom 20 per cent of the holdings account for only 3 per cent of the land while the top 10 per cent account for over 35 per cent. The Gini concentration ratio is 0.5. In the other six countries the distribution is less equal. For example, the Gini concentration ratios of the distribution of landholding for Pakistan, India and the Philippines have been estimated to be around 0.6.[2]

None of these countries made any significant progress towards redistribution of land during the periods considered. For those countries for which information is available no significant trend towards reducing inequality can be found. Pakistan, Philippines and Sri Lanka initiated some land reform measures in the early 1970s. Although our studies were not able fully to take into account their effects, it is reasonably clear by now that the redistributive consequences of these measures are likely to be marginal.

The continuation of the highly unequal ownership of land during a period of rapid demographic growth has resulted in increased landlessness and near-landlessness. Due to a curious lack of enthusiasm on the part of the statistical authorities in these countries it is very difficult to obtain a time series on the number of landless workers. In those cases where information is available, e.g. in Bangladesh and parts of India, a marked trend towards increased landlessness can be discerned.

II. CAUSAL MECHANISMS

A salient characteristic of the countries we have studied is that many of the resources needed for development are at hand, unutilised or poorly utilised. Foremost among these is the intelligence,ingenuity and effort of the labour force itself. It has long been known that part, usually a small part, of the rural work force often is openly unemployed, particularly during the slack season in regions where multiple cropping is not practised. In addition, a larger part of the work force may be underemployed in the sense that it is engaged in tasks with a very low level of productivity. More important, perhaps, than unemployment and underemployment is the low productivity and occasionally low intensity of work arising from the poor motivation, poor health and injustice that is found in most rural areas. The exploitation and inequality to which the majority of the rural population is subjected is demoralising, engenders resentment and stifles initiative and creativity. The effect is not only to lower current output below its potential but to reduce the capacity and willingness of the population to innovate. Where inequality is so severe that infants of the poor suffer from protein malnutrition, intelligence is permanently impaired and their creative talent is destroyed. In societies where material deprivation is less acute, effects on initiative and innovation may be similar because of the psychological consequences of a warped incentive system and the sociological consequences of a social structure which ensures that most of the economic surplus is captured by a small minority.

Labour is not the only resource that is poorly utilised; in many countries land and other natural resources are not efficiently exploited. Especially on the larger farms, the length of the fallow period is excessively long, the degree of cropping intensity is too low and the amount of land in natural pastures is high. At the same time, many of the smallest farmers are forced to over-exploit their land, with the result that useful land is destroyed through erosion and the exhaustion of soil fertility. Just as the economic system in the countries we have studied results in poor use (and even destruction) of part of its human resources, so too it results in poor use (and even destruction) of part of its natural resources.

Underutilisation of labour and land often is accompanied by underutilisation of capital. Large irrigation facilities are not used to capacity; irrigation canals and drainage ditches are allowed to fall into disrepair; fish ponds are permitted to become overgrown with weeds; mechanical equipment becomes inoperative because of a lack of spare parts. Furthermore, much of the savings potential of the peasantry remains untapped, and hence the rate of accumulation of capital remains lower than necessary.

Latent within these inefficiencies and inequities are possibilities for higher output, faster growth and greater equality. This potential for rural development, however, has lain dormant. Instead of growing prosperity for those most in need there has been impoverishment. The crucial question is why.

It certainly is not the case that the increasing poverty of the poor is due to general stagnation in Asia, or, worse, economic decline. On the contrary, all but one of the seven countries surveyed has enjoyed a rise in average incomes in recent years, and in some instances the rise has been quite rapid; only in Bangladesh have average incomes fallen. Excluding Bangladesh, between 1960 and 1973, GNP per head increased between 1.3 per cent a year (in India) and 3.9 per cent (in Malaysia). Thus it is the pattern of growth in Asia that has been most unsatisfactory rather than the rate of growth. The pattern has been such that despite a fairly rapid increase in average income per head, poverty in rural areas has tended to rise. It is tempting to argue that one reason for this is that the growth has been of a type consistent with slow growth of agriculture. The basic point that is being made, however, is that in a period of increasing prosperity, poverty in rural areas has not diminished and probably has increased.

The claim that the growing poverty of Asia is due to a world food shortage or to a failure of food production in Asia to keep up with the expanding population is untenable. If one examines our seven countries individually, it transpires that, in the period covered by our studies, in only one of them did population expand faster than domestic food production. This was in Bangladesh where, as we have seen, even GNP *per capita* has been falling. In India population and food production have grown at the same rate, while cereal production has expanded faster than the population;[3] in Pakistan food production may have grown fractionally faster than the population and cereal production significantly faster. In all the other countries studied food production clearly has increased faster than the population, and in some countries, notably Sri Lanka and Malaysia, the difference in growth rates has been very large.

The answer to why poverty has increased has more to do with the structure of the economy than its rate of growth. One structural feature common to all the countries studied is a high degree of inequality. Data from the six countries on which information is available suggest that in the economy as a whole the richest 20 per cent of households typically receive about half the income, whereas the poorest 40 per cent receive between 12 and 18 per cent of total income. The bottom 20 per cent fare even worse, of course, receiving about 7 per cent of the income in the least inegalitarian country (Bangladesh) and merely 3.8 per cent in one of the most inegalitarian countries (Philippines).

The degree of income inequality in rural areas is somewhat less than in the urban areas and, hence, less unequal than the average for the economy. None the less, the degree of inequality is considerable. According to the available data, rural India is the least inegalitarian while rural Malaysia and the Philippines are the most. Little emphasis should be placed on these differences, however, as the data are not very precise and in the case of India in particular it is widely believed that the data understate the extent of inequality.

The counterpart to the compression of the income on the poor is the concentration of the economic surplus in a very few hands. The disposal of this surplus, in turn, largely determines the pace and composition of economic growth. The preferences of the upper-income groups as between present consumption and savings will affect the rate of accumulation. The pattern of demand, itself strongly influenced by the distribution of income, will determine in large part the sectors into which investment flows. And the set of relative factor prices which confront those who invest the surplus will have an effect on the methods of production that are used, the amount of employment that is generated, the productivity of that employment and the distribution of income.

The structure of factor markets is such that the unequal distribution of income arising from an unequal distribution of productive assets is reinforced by the operations of the price mechanism. Those who have access to the organised capital market are able to obtain finance capital for investment on very favourable terms.[4] Indeed, when nominal rates of interest are adjusted for inflation, the real rate of interest paid by large investors often is negative. This introduces a strong bias in favour of investment in the more capital-intensive sectors and in the more capital-intensive methods of production. As a result, the demand for labour is lower than it would otherwise have been. Paradoxically, the relatively high productivity of labour associated with the more mechanised processes may lead to higher wages for those who secure employment in the sector, thereby further reducing the demand for labour.[5]

This pattern of investment is accentuated in countries where a system of protection is combined with a foreign exchange rate that is overvalued and import permits for foreign equipment consequently must be allocated through a rationing device of some sort.[6] The contrived cheapening of imported goods relative to domestic labour introduces an additional bias in favour of (foreign) capital intensity, and tends to raise the share of profits in national income while reducing the demand for labour.

The capital markets operate in such a way that a small minority of the labour force is equipped with excessively capital-intensive techniques, given the relative availabilities of investible resources and labour. At the same time, the majority of the labour force (in urban as well as in rural areas) is forced to work with techniques which are insufficiently capital-intensive. As a result, the productivity and incomes of the majority are exceptionally low compared to those employed in the so-called modern, capital-intensive sector. Crude guesstimates from Indonesia, for example, suggest that in the modern sector it costs about $5,000 to equip each additional worker. Expansion of employment in this sector provides for about 12 per cent of the new entrants into the labour force and absorbs over 70 per cent of the surplus allocated to investment. As a result, the investible surplus available for those who enter the informal urban sector and rural occupations is less than $300 per worker.

Price-cum-rationing mechanisms are also present in other parts of the economy. In fact most markets for intermediate goods and services operate in a fashion parallel to that of the capital market. For instance, electric power typically is distributed highly unevenly, many rural areas being excluded from the national network. Efficient transportation services are available to only a relatively few producers, again many rural areas being isolated from the main currents of commerce. Within the rural areas, technical assistance is concentrated on the large farmers and research programmes are often oriented toward their needs. Finally, even the labour market operates to the disadvantage of the poor, since monopsonistic elements are present in many localities, often associated with a high degree of concentration of land ownership.[7]

The initially high degree of inequality of income and wealth, the concentration of the economic surplus in a few enterprises and households, and the fragmented allocative mechanisms constitute a socio-economic context in which powerful dynamic forces tend to perpetuate and even accentuate low standards of living of a significant proportion of the rural population. Four such forces, or processes occuring through time, should be mentioned.

First, there is the accumulation of capital in the private sector. The volume of private investment is a relatively low proportion of the economic surplus appropriated by those who control the national wealth. Although some capital formation occurs in rural areas, much of it is channelled into the urban areas, notwithstanding the fact that in the countries studied the urban population accounts for as little as 10 per cent of the total in Bangladesh and about 30 per cent in the most urbanised country, Malaysia. This 'urban bias'[8] in the pattern of investment often takes the form, as we have seen, of highly capital-intensive projects in which the share of wages in value added is relatively low. As a result, the rate of growth of employment in the capital-intensive sector is slow, sometimes not even as fast as the rate of growth of the labour force. In the Philippines, for example, the proportion of the labour force engaged in manufacturing fell from 13 per cent in 1957 to less than 10 per cent a decade and a half later.[9]

Those unable to find a job in the capital-intensive activities must seek a livelihood either in the urban informal sector or in rural areas, or become openly unemployed. If the labour force entering these categories grows faster than the rate of capital formation in the informal sector and rural areas combined, there is likely to be a tendency to fall of the real incomes of the most vulnerable workers in the most vulnerable sectors.

Next, these pressures are likely to be exacerbated by investment trends in the public sector. The reason for this is that in the mixed economies of Asia public capital formation essentially supports private sector activities, particularly the large and capital-intensive enterprises. This, in turn, arises from the fact that the groups on which the government relies for support are the same groups which possess most of the wealth of the country, supply the majority of technicians and administrators and provide the leadership of the army and the dominant political alignments. Economic and political influence are closely interwoven: those who possess purchasing power also possess political power.

Then, the process of technical change may tend to have a labour-saving bias in the activities in which most capital accumulation occurs. Part of the explanation for this is that the pattern of technical innovation is certain to be influenced by the set of relative factor prices which large investors confront. It has already been shown that these factor prices encourage the adoption of relatively capital-intensive methods which economise on labour. A second reason is that most of the Asian economies under study are dependent for much of their innovation on imported foreign technology. This technology was developed in economies where labour is scarce and capital is abundant, and hence their importation into economies where the opposite conditions prevail is likely to diminish still further the number of jobs created for each ten thousand dollars of investment.

Consequently, in the sectors and activities where most of the capital accumulation occurs—in manufacturing, on the large mechanised farms, in port, airport and highway development—there is a danger that technical change will exhibit a pattern that is increasingly labour-displacing. In the remainder of the economy, however, where the majority of the labour force is employed, the investible surplus is small and producers are forced by circumstances to seek land and capital-saving technologies. At times this process may be carried to such an extent that the ratio of land and capital to labour begins to fall and a period of increasing poverty, declining labour productivity and 'agricultural involution' begins.[10]

Whether or not this happens, and to what extent, depends of course upon our final dynamic process: the rate of growth of the population and associated demographic phenomena. Given the structure of the economy as it has been described and the resulting nature of the processes of capital formation and innovation, the faster the pace of expansion of the population and labour force, the stronger will be the tendency for the standard of living of some groups or classes to fall. Alas, the available estimates indicate, without exception, that the present rates of population growth in the seven Asian countries are high. The slowest estimated rate of demographic expansion is 2 per cent a year (in Indonesia), while the fastest is about 3 per cent (in Pakistan and the Philippines).

It is important to underline, however, that the cause of increasing poverty in Asia is not an alleged population explosion. Rapid population growth is merely a contributing factor. The basic causes are the unequal ownership of land and other productive assets, allocative mechanisms which discriminate in favour of the owners of wealth, and a pattern of capital accumulation and technical innovation which is biased against labour.

Because of the rate and pattern of investment and technical change the number of workers that can be readily absorbed in urban areas and in non-farm rural activities is relatively small—far smaller than the increase in the work force. Agricultural production is characterised by diminishing returns to labour, which of course in principle could be offset by high rates of accumulation and innovation. Unfortunately, however, investment in agriculture has been relatively low, especially on the small farms, yet the sector has been forced to retain a large proportion of the yearly increase in the labour force.

In consequence, the tendency toward diminishing returns and falling output per worker has not always been compensated by rising investment. As population densities and the man – land ratio have increased, the level and share of rents have risen, while the wage share, wage rates and the number of days employed per person have tended to decline. That is, at the going terms of agricultural remuneration, the demand for labour has increased less rapidly than the supply and hence the standard of living has fallen of those who depend on work as a source of income. This has affected some plantation workers, unskilled landless agricultural labourers, pure tenants and some small landowners who have to supplement their income by engaging in paid labour.

Thus it is that in a world that is far from being perfectly competitive, a rise in national income per head and in food production per head is quite compatible, not only with greater relative inequality, but with greater hunger and falling incomes for the poorest members of society. The study of Asian economic development indicates that the initial distribution of wealth and income has a decisive influence over the pattern of growth and hence over the rate of amelioration or deterioration in the standard of living of the lowest-income groups. Furthermore, given the initial conditions, it is difficult to change the distribution of income by manipulating standard policy instruments—tax, subsidy and expenditure levels, exchange rates and trade controls, monetary variables, etc. It follows from this that a 'grow now, redistribute later' strategy is not a valid option in most countries; it is necessary first to 'get the structure right'.

III. DEFICIENCIES OF FORMAL MODELS

The foregoing suggests that the economic processes that produce poverty are too complex to be described adequately by a formal model consisting of a system of a large number of equations. The structure of a realistic model would be extremely complicated. Even if such a model could be set out in mathematical terms its numerical application would be virtually impossible in view of the immense difficulty of measuring all the parameters.

This, however, is not to suggest that formal models have no role to play in promoting an understanding of poverty and in planning for its eradication. What clearly is not feasible is to develop a comprehensive model of poverty that would explain all the causative factors and enable one to trace the results of all possible policies. On the other hand, some specific aspects of the process can be illuminated in important ways by the explicit specification of the major interrelationships in quantitative terms. Especially in planning for the reduction of poverty, relatively simple formal models may be able to shed light on the interaction between particular actions and the final outcomes in terms of changes in the magnitude and composition of poverty.

To achieve these goals of providing a partial explanation of poverty and indicating the impact of policy measures on the eradication of poverty the formal models must incorporate the crucially important variables and relationships. Here we can only highlight a few of these that are often omitted from such models.

It seems reasonable to ask to what extent have economists been able to explain the ugly facts we have described above by their theorising, including theorising done while constructing formal models. Despite the time, energy and ingenuity that have been lavished on theories of economic development and on the design of formal models intended either to describe or help governments plan the development process, it appears that not as much light as one would hope has been shed so far on why poor people remain poor. Perhaps one reason for this is that the building blocks of most theories and models are faulty.

Our empirical work has demonstrated that poverty is associated with particular classes or groups in the community, e.g. landless agricultural labourers, village artisans, plantation workers, etc. Yet most theories and models are couched in terms of atomistic households in a classless society. This neoclassical assumption is closely associated with an assumption of universal harmony of interests.

We do not believe it is possible to get very far in understanding the problems of the Third World until it is more widely accepted that there are classes in society and that the interests of the various classes are often in conflict. Posing the issue in this way forces one to examine the distribution of wealth (a variable neglected in most models) and then to view the distribution of income as closely related to the underlying distribution of assets. A chain of association is thereby established between class structure, the ownership of wealth and the distribution of income.[11]

Such a framework has several advantages. First, it encourages investigators interested in problems of income distribution to abandon models framed in terms of decile rankings and the like, and to substitute instead classes or groups of persons. If it is true that certain types of growth processes reduce incomes absolutely, then this must operate through identifiable groups, classes or persons in comparable situations, not through deciles except as a by-product. That is, changes in the share of a particular decile reflect possibly offsetting movements in the fate of heterogeneous groups who happen to be represented in that decile.

Second, the proposed framework would encourage the investigator to confront the awkward question of the function of the state in a class society. Implicit in most models is the assumption that the state is a neutral and benevolent arbiter attempting to maximise a social welfare function. One cannot avoid concluding from the evidence of our empirical studies, however, either that the arbiter is woefully ignorant or that economists have a rather naive theory of the state. Again, if analytical methods are to help us understand what is going on, we shall have to revise our thinking on the behaviour of the state.

If the state were seen as an endogenous element in the economy, an institution which reflects the underlying social forces and structure of production, and not an external agent enjoying free will, the investigator would be encouraged to examine other phenomena in a new light. For example, prices are commonly regarded as a product of a market clearing process in a competitive environment. True, monopolistic features and other 'distortions' are acknowledged, but these are treated as anomalies to be corrected by the state. In the framework we have proposed, in contrast, the possibility exists for a rational state to intervene actively in the process of price formation, not to eliminate 'distortions' but to create them.

In several models, notably that of Adelman and Robinson, the extent and location of poverty are strongly influenced by changes in the agricultural terms of trade.[12] In other work, including some done by one of us,[13] emphasis is placed on differences in ease of access to resources by different groups or classes, and in particular on variations in the set of relative factor prices which different groups confront. These differences in relative prices are used to account for the techniques of production that are adopted, the pattern of innovation and the resulting changes in the distribution of income among classes. What we are now suggesting is (i) that prices should be incorporated into formal models concerned with poverty, (ii) that provision should be made for the possibility that different groups will face different sets of prices and (iii) that the state should be treated as a 'price maker' with a class bias which determines who faces what prices.

Such an approach to the problem of development is likely to lead us to alter our conception of the nature of poverty. Many economists work with an absolute income concept and this leads them naturally to think in terms of minimum income requirements, poverty lines, basic needs and all that. Others view poverty in terms of relative low income and hence focus on the degree of inequality, shares in income of the bottom deciles of the population, Gini coefficients and the like. Perhaps it would be better, however, to work with a structural definition of poverty, in which poverty is regarded as a product of a social system and reflects differences in access of various groups to sources of economic and political power.

This view of the nature of poverty would sever the link once and for all between, on the one hand, the extent of poverty (and its direction of change) and, on the other, the level of average income (and its rate of growth). A preoccupation with questions of income inequality would remain, but these issues would be examined within an analytical framework in which the distribution of productive wealth, the resulting class hierarchy of society and the behaviour of the state play leading roles. Dynamic processes—the appropriation and disposal of the investible surplus, the pattern of private and state investment, the speed and nature of technical innovation—could then be explained, at least in part, in terms of the fundamental characteristics of the economy.

Above all, a structural definition of poverty focuses attention on where one should look for remedies. The provision of welfare services and income transfers are ruled out because they do not remove the underlying causes of poverty. Efforts devoted to expanding the output of allegedly key commodities, e.g. food, are exposed as being inadequate because of the lack of connection between changes in production and changes in purchasing power in the hands of the poor. Thus our conceptualisation of poverty makes it clearer why both micro- and macro-economic tinkering are almost certain to fail. The remedy lies in structural change, in changing the distribution of productive wealth (and consequently the distribution of economic power) and in increasing the participation of the poor in decision-making (and consequently enabling them to exercise political power).

NOTES AND REFERENCES

* This chapter was written jointly with Azizur Rahman Khan.
  1. See Keith Griffin and Azizur Rahman Khan (eds), *Poverty and Landlessness in Rural Asia* (Geneva: ILO, mimeo., 1976). Much of this chapter consists of extensive quotation from Chapter One of the above and an attempt to summarise the main empirical findings of the other chapters. A revised version was published by the ILO under the same title in 1977.
  2. These estimates, for 1960, are reported in IBRD, *Land Reform*, World Bank Paper, Rural Development Series, (July 1974).
  3. In the period 1956–7 to 1973–4 agricultural output per head increased 1.3

per cent a year in Bihar, 3.2 per cent in the Punjab, 1.0 per cent in Tamil Nadu and 1.4 per cent in Uttar Pradesh. That is, *per capita* agricultural output increased significantly in all of the states studied, yet the data in Table 10 indicate that only in Tamil Nadu did the incidence of rural poverty fail to increase. Thus it is unlikely that the major explanation for the persistence and even increase in poverty is slow agricultural growth.

4. See, for example, Ronald I. McKinnon, *Money and Capital in Economic Development* (Washington: Brookings Institution, 1973).
5. Thus the sequence is (i) 'cheap' finance capital leads to (ii) adoption of 'excessively' mechanised techniques which, in turn, results in (iii) high productivity of labour. This both provokes a demand for and facilitates the payment of (iv) higher wages which then leads to (v) a second-round reduction in the quantity of labour demanded.
6. See I. M. D. Little, T. Scitovsky and M. Scott, *Industry and Trade in Some Developing Countries* (London: Oxford University Press, 1970).
7. See Keith Griffin, *Land Concentration and Rural Poverty* (London: Macmillan, 1976).
8. See Michael Lipton, *Why Poor People Stay Poor: Urban Bias in World Development* (London: Temple Smith, 1977).
9. ILO, *Sharing in Development: A Programme of Employment, Equity and Growth for the Philippines* (1974) Tables 77 and 78, pp. 433 and 434.
10. Clifford Geertz, *Agricultural Involution: The Process of Ecological Change in Indonesia* (University of California Press, 1968).
11. One of the virtues of the accounting system advocated by Graham Pyatt and Erik Thorbecke is that it does focus on particular groups of households and the associated asset and income distribution. See their *Planning Techniques for a Better Future* (Geneva: ILO, 1976).
12. I. Adelman and S. Robinson, *Income Distribution Policies in Developing Countries: A Case Study of Korea* (London: Oxford University Press, 1977).
13. Keith Griffin, *The Political Economy of Agrarian Change* (London: Macmillan, 1974).

Appendix to Chapter 6. The efficiency wage hypothesis: another fancy model

An economic case can be made that increased provision to the poor of certain items conventionally classified as consumption could result in higher labour productivity and output. The supply of clean water, elementary education, adequate nutrition, preventive health services and sufficient shelter and clothing to protect people from the worst effects of the weather is both an objective of development and a means for its attainment. Expenditures on these and other items will be directly productive in so far as they increase the ability and willingness of people to work harder, for more hours and with greater enthusiasm, initiative and innovativeness. This, in turn, could occur partly because greater provision of these goods and services would increase the strength and endurance of workers while on the job, partly because it would lower morbidity and hence reduce the number of days lost from work, and partly because of the psychological effects on morale.

Put in these rather general terms the existence of some sort of a connection between increased consumption and higher productivity, with causality flowing from the former to the latter, probably would command a consensus. The specification of a precise functional relationship, however, is another matter. Two decades ago Harvey Leibenstein published a paper on 'The Theory of Underemployment in Backward Economies'[1] in which he postulated a relationship between wages, units of work and productivity. This hypothesis was relatively neglected until recently, when it was dubbed 'the efficiency wage hypothesis' by Professor Stiglitz[2] and used by Professor Mirrlees as the keystone in his formulation of 'A Pure Theory of Underdeveloped Economies'.[3] A recent paper by Bliss and Stern consists of an elaboration of the Mirrlees version of the hypothesis and a discussion of its empirical validity.[4]

I. THE PROBLEM POSED

Bliss and Stern are concerned with the possibility 'that the link from consumption to productivity exerts an important influence on wages' and that this 'might provide the explanation for the apparent tendency for wages to hold up even in the presence of large reserves of unemployed labour.' Two questions immediately arise from the way the problem is posed. First, are there in fact 'large reserves' of unemployed labour? Second, is it true that wages tend to remain constant when the ordinary forces of supply and demand would lead one to expect them to fall? Since the authors' analysis is presented as applying to rural areas we shall refer to evidence from these areas only.

First, for several years results of empirical research have been available indicating that unemployment in rural areas is relatively low. The evidence assembled by David Turnham suggests that the wholly unemployed in rural areas typically are about 3 to 4 per cent of the labour force, although they can be much higher than this, as in Sri Lanka.[5] Furthermore, almost all of the rural unemployment in underdeveloped countries arises from the seasonal demand for labour in agriculture. Colin Clark and Margaret Haswell published estimates years ago of the monthly demand for labour in agriculture as a percentage of the available labour supply. Their data indicate that in China, India, Egypt, parts of Iraq and in Ghana there is virtually full employment during the period of peak demand but that during the slack season the demand for labour can be very low.[6] More recent work in India[7] and Egypt[8] confirms the view that even in these densely populated countries there is very little unemployment in rural areas during the most active months of the year.

Second, there is equally abundant evidence that wage rates in rural areas are highly variable. At least since the time of Bent Hansen's study of Egypt[9] it has been known that wages fluctuate over the agricultural season, both in nominal and real terms, rising and falling with shifts in demand. More recently it has become apparent that in several countries in Asia the real wage rate has shown a tendency to decline. For example, in the Philippines the real daily wage in agriculture exhibited a clear and sharp downward trend between 1957 and 1974.[10] In Sri Lanka real wages in the plantation sector fell continuously between 1968 and 1972.[11] In Bangladesh, real wages in agriculture were lower in 1975 than they were in 1949.[12] Furthermore, even nominal wage rates in rural areas have been known to fall; the fall in real wages is not always due entirely to rising prices of wage goods. For instance, nominal wages fell in Bangladesh between 1949 and 1955 and from 1964 to 1965.[13] Earlier, in Burma, the money wage of ploughmen fell by nearly 20 per cent from 1912 to 1922 and real wages by as much as 35 per cent.[14] Outside Asia, real wages in Egypt fell rather steadily between 1951 and 1955 and again between 1966 and 1974, while nominal wages fell frequently between 1951 and 1961.[15]

Thus it would appear that the point of departure for Bliss and Stern is unfortunate. The readily available data contradict their beliefs that in rural areas there are 'large reserves of unemployed labour' and that wages successfully resist the downward pressure these large reserve create. There is a great danger that their hypothesis is designed to explain phenomena which do not exist.

II. THE EFFICIENCY WAGE HYPOTHESIS

Let us suspend judgement on this, however, until we consider the implications of their hypothesis in some detail. Bliss and Stern assume that all income is spent on food and that food consumption can be measured in terms of calories. They then postulate that the number of effective hours provided by a worker in a day of given clock hours is a function of his consumption of calories and in particular that there is a region of increasing returns to consumption. In this manner a chain of connections is established between the daily wage rate, consumption of calories, effective labour inputs and productivity. The consumption – productivity relationship is regarded in much the same way as others have regarded the production function of the firm: the worker is a machine which takes in calories and emits effective hours.

On the basis of this reasoning the authors construct a theory of wages. They examine the case of a single employer hiring workers as well as the case where there are many employers. They also consider two kinds of workers, landless labourers (type 0) and small peasant landowners who supplement their income by engaging in part-time paid employment (type 1).

Bliss and Stern reach four broad conclusions. First, it often pays the employer to offer a wage to workers above that which would be determined by the ordinary forces of supply and demand, since in this way he can take account of the 'fact' that, over a certain range, higher wages result in greater efficiency and lower costs. That is, a single landlord enjoying a monopsony position, far from exploiting labour, would pay a wage even higher than would prevail under perfectly competitive conditions. Second, the wage rate in villages consisting entirely of landless labourers (call it W_0) would be higher than the wage rate in villages consisting entirely of small peasants (call it W_1). Third, the income of landless labourers ($= W_0$) in villages where they are the sole type of worker would be larger than the income of small peasants in villages where *they* constitute the entire labour force. That is, $W_0 > W_1 + C_1$, where C_1 is the consumption obtained by small peasant landowners from working on their own farms. In villages dominated by a single employer where the two types of labour coexist, $W_0 = W_1 + C_1$. Fourth, in villages where both type 0 and type 1 workers coexist, no landless workers would be employed until the supply of type 1 workers had run out. But if there is competition among employers the wages of the two types of workers would then become similar.

Unfortunately, the deductions from the theory are no more persuasive than the premises on which it is based. We have already seen that wages do fluctuate in rural areas. If both real and nominal wages of agricultural labourers can and do fall in a country as poor and badly nourished as Bangladesh, the applicability of the efficiency wage hypothesis must be very limited indeed. Furthermore, if the model of Bliss and Stern were correct one would expect that, *ceteris paribus*, wage rates would be higher where the labour force is 'captive' and has a low rate of turnover, as on plantations, than in areas where arable agriculture is practised, as in regions growing grains. Yet the data indicate that wages are no higher on plantations than elsewhere; if anything, they are lower. After all, it is the plantation workers in Sri Lanka who often are on the verge of starvation, not the landless labourers in the paddy-growing areas.

Within the arable areas the theory seems to imply that the wages of permanent workers would exceed those of casual workers. Bliss and Stern appear to believe that their observations in a village in western Uttar Pradesh in the winter season of 1974–5 support this aspect of the theory. Once again, however, the data I have seen indicate that the opposite almost always is the case, i.e. casual workers are paid more than permanent ones.[16] In effect, permanent workers receive a lower daily wage rate in exchange for security of employment.

One peculiar implication of Bliss and Stern's hypothesis is that the incomes of small peasants often would be no larger than those of landless labourers and in some circumstances would be lower. That is, under some assumptions peasant income derived from cultivating their own farms would be insufficient to compensate for the difference between the low wage paid to peasant (type 1) workers and the higher wage paid to landless (type 0) workers. [17] Under these circumstances one might expect to observe cases of small landowners selling or even giving their land to large landlords in exchange for a promise from the latter to employ them as a landless agricultural labourer. As far as I am aware, no transactions motivated by theoretical considerations of this nature are reported in the vast literature on village India—although reports of distress sales of land by peasants to landlords are of course common.

The model has been extended by the authors to incorporate several other topics of interest, [18] but perhaps enough has been said to cast doubt on the validity of the general approach. I must emphasise, however, that I am sceptical only of the model; I agree with the broad proposition that in principle increased consumption of food and other items can raise the productivity of impoverished workers. The analysis of Bliss and Stern suffers from the fact that it is embedded in an individualistic, market framework. Surely, if labour productivity is a function of consumption this is an argument either for a redistribution of income and wealth (and hence of consumption) within a capitalist system or for determining the distribution of consumption on the basis of collective decisions. There is no reason whatever to think that in an economy in which average incomes are low and the distribution of income is highly unequal the market will ensure that all employed workers receive an income high enough to ensure their efficiency and adequate nutrition.

The benefits of increased consumption are difficult to isolate and quantify and evidently cannot be captured through market processes. This is a clear instance of 'externalities'. Moreover, as Bliss and Stern demonstrate, the benefits from extra consumption are likely to be of a long-term character. Thus one must agree with them that the efficiency wage hypothesis 'has no strong relevance'. Indeed, the theory is a complete failure: it cannot account for underemployment, it does not explain how wages are determined in rural areas and it certainly cannot be used to construct 'a pure theory of underdeveloped economies'.

III. POVERTY LINES AND THE NATURE OF POVERTY

Having rejected the theory, admittedly in less trenchant terms than have I, Bliss and Stern discuss the work of others which relates poverty lines to nutritional requirements. In particular they are critical of Bardhan's attempt to compare the proportion of people in poverty in rural India in

1960–1 with the proportion in 1968–9.[19] Bliss and Stern demonstrate that a 20 per cent reduction in minimum requirements (which is reasonable given the uncertainty of the figures) would reduce by half the estimated number of people below the line. They then suggest that attempts to calculate the number in poverty 'have rather little value'.

This suggestion, it seems to me, betrays an extraordinary amount of confusion. Part of the confusion arises from the physiological view of poverty taken by Bliss and Stern. There appears to be an underlying theme throughout their paper that if only enough calories could be stuffed into people, poverty would disappear. This of course is nonsense. Poverty is a sociological, not a physiological phenomenon. Its measurement has nothing to do with calories as such; rather, as Théron de Montaugé told us a century ago, 'poverty is measured by comparisons.'[20] That is, the higher the general standard of living, the higher the poverty line. Thus whether or not Bardhan's budget provided for too few or too many calories for nutritional adequacy is irrelevant; all that matters is whether his poverty line makes sociological sense in the Indian context.

In my opinion what is needed is not criticism of Bardhan's pioneering research but an extension of it. Poverty lines undoubtedly have their limitations as an analytical device but they can be useful if four conditions are satisfied.

First, whenever a single poverty line is used in a country it should be culturally specific and no attempt should be made to reflect imaginary universal standards. In many cases culturally specific poverty lines may be related to nutritional norms, but there is nothing intrinsic to the concept which requires that they be so.

Second, there are advantages in working with more than one poverty line. Calculations of the incidence of poverty under alternative assumptions about the poverty line enable one to obtain an indication of the distribution of income among those in poverty. The so-called 'poverty gap' measure devised by Amartya Sen is another way of taking into account the distance of people below a single line.[21]

Third, poverty lines should be disaggregated. That is, poverty could be defined in terms of having at least W number of calories in the diet, X years of education, Y yards of clothing material and Z rupees of income. People may be poor in one dimension and not so poor in another and a disaggregated approach of the type proposed would enable one to detect this. Moreover, disaggregation is essential if a country wishes to follow a 'basic needs' approach to development.

Finally, measurement of the incidence of poverty—in multiple dimensions and using more than one poverty line for each—should be repeated periodically. The main reason for using poverty lines is that one can thereby determine whether the proportion of the population in poverty is rising or falling over time. For example, the fact that Bardhan may have overestimated the proportion in poverty by a half—if he did— is less important than the fact that the incidence of rural poverty, however defined, increased. Only if governments are able to monitor poverty will they know if the policies introduced to alleviate it are having the desired effect. A great advantage of poverty lines is that they represent a relatively easy way of finding out what one needs to know.

If one accepts this argument, then contrary to Bliss and Stern there is a need for further research to refine the crude methods employed by the pioneers. One way of organising this, and no doubt there are other ways, would be under the four headings discussed above. The essential point, however, is that the work be done, for it is likely to be of considerable value to those who wish to understand poverty in order to do something about it.

NOTES AND REFERENCES

1. *Journal of Political Economy* (Apr. 1957).
2. Joseph E. Stiglitz, 'The Efficiency Wage Hypothesis, Surplus Labour, and the Distribution of Income in L.D.C.s', *Oxford Economic Papers* (July 1976).
3. James A. Mirrlees, 'A Pure Theory of Underdeveloped Economies', in Lloyd G. Reynolds (ed.), *Agriculture in Development Theory* (Yale University Press, 1975).
4. Christopher Bliss and Nicholas Stern, 'Productivity, Wages and Nutrition in the Context of Less Developed Countries', a paper presented to the 5th World Congress of the International Economic Association, Tokyo, Japan (Sep. 1977).
5. David Turnham, *The Employment Problem in Less Developed Countries: A Review of the Evidence* (OECD, 1971) p. 76.
6. Colin Clark and Margaret Haswell, *The Economics of Subsistence Agriculture*, 2nd ed. (London: Macmillan, 1966) p. 130.
7. M. Paglin, ' "Surplus" Agricultural Labour and Development', *American Economic Review* (Sep. 1965); for a careful study of Tamil Nadu, India see B. H. Farmer, (ed.), *Green Revolution?* (London: Macmillan, 1977) Table 14.5, p. 213 and Fig. 14.2, pp. 214–15. Also see C. H. Hanumantha Rao, *Technological Change and Distribution of Gains in Indian Agriculture*, Macmillan of India, 1975, p. 119.
8. Bent Hansen, 'Employment and Wages in Rural Egypt', *American Economic Review* (June 1969).
9. Ibid. On India, see C. H. Hanumantha Rao, op. cit., p. 120.
10. A. R. Khan, 'Growth and Inequality in the Rural Philippines', in ILO,

Poverty and Landlessness in Rural Asia (1977) Table 98, p. 244 and Fig. 11, p. 246.

11. E. L. H. Lee, 'Rural Poverty in Sri Lanka, 1963–1973', ILO, op. cit., Table 63, p. 167.

12. A. R. Khan, 'Poverty and Inequality in Rural Bangladesh', ILO, op. cit., Table 50, p. 151.

13. Ibid.

14. James C. Scott, *The Moral Economy of the Peasant: Rebellion and Subsistence in Southeast Asia* (Yale University Press, 1976) p. 75 citing Michael Adas, *The Burma Delta: Economic Development and Social Change on an Asian Rice Frontier* (University of Wisconsin Press, 1974) p. 152.

15. Samir Radwan, 'The Impact of Agrarian Reform on Rural Egypt (1952–75)', ILO, Geneva, WEP Working Paper (Jan. 1977) Table 3.2, p. 29.

16. See for example, Government of India, *Agricultural Labour in India: Report of the Second Enquiry*, Vol. 1, (1960); P. S. Sanghvi, *Surplus Manpower in Agriculture and Economic Development* (Bombay: Asia Publishing House, 1969); Jan Breman, *Patronage and Exploitation: Changing Agrarian Relations in South Gujarat, India*, (University of California Press, 1974) pp. 126–9.

17. It is possible to observe that average wages of type 1 labour are sometimes lower than the average wage of type 0 workers. This is because peasants are in the labour market for fewer days than landless workers during the peak seasons, having to devote their effort to their own farms. Task-specific wage rates, however, are the same for both types of workers.

18. The paper includes separate sections on worker's choice, the shadow wage rate (where, following Stiglitz, op. cit., they conclude that it is negative!), employment subsidies and choice of family size.

19. See P. K. Bardhan, 'On the Incidence of Poverty in Rural India of the Sixties', *Economic and Political Weekly*, (Feb. 1973).

20. Louis Théron de Montaugé *L'Agriculture et les Classes Rurales dans le Pays Toulousain depuis le Milieu du XVIIIe siècle*, (1869) quoted in Eugen Weber, *Peasants into Frenchmen: The Modernization of Rural France, 1870–1914* (London: Chatto and Windus, 1977) p. 22.

21. Amartya Sen, 'Poverty: An Ordinal Approach to Measurement', *Econometrica* (Mar. 1976).

7. Increasing poverty and changing ideas about development strategies

In the Third World as a whole the rate of growth in the last quarter century or so has been unprecedented. Never before have so many poor countries—containing such a large proportion of those who are inadequately fed, clothed and housed—enjoyed such a period of rapid and sustained expansion of output. Yet despite this growth of production the problems of widespread poverty seem to have remained as great as ever. The rise in aggregate production does not seem to have been matched by a corresponding rise in the income of the poor.

Evidence of the persistence of poverty takes many forms. For example, the number of those unable to read and write has increased. The employment problem has remained intractable and in some areas may have become worse. Hunger and malnutrition are chronic and in parts of Asia and Africa periodic famines stalk the land. Perhaps most distressing is evidence, still incomplete but sufficiently strong that it can no longer be ignored, that in many countries the standard of living of the poorest members of the population has been falling absolutely.

As indicated in the previous chapter, a series of empirical studies of trends in living standards in the rural areas of Asia recently has been completed.[1] These studies, it will be recalled, covered four states of India (the Punjab, Uttar Pradesh, Bihar and Tamil Nadu), plus Pakistan, Bangladesh, Sri Lanka, Malaysia, Indonesia and the Philippines. The studies, thus, provide an indicator of what has been happening in countries which account for about 70 per cent of the rural population of the Third World.

The available data from Asia were organised in three different ways. First, in most cases it was possible to construct a poverty line, based upon a partly arbitrary nutritional standard, and measure changes in the proportion of the rural population in poverty.[2] In all but two of the eight cases where this was possible it was found that the percentage of the rural population below the poverty line has tended to increase; in the other two cases the percentage was roughly constant.[3]

Second, in other cases it was possible to calculate changes over time in the real incomes of decile or quintile groups. Again it was found that the real incomes of the lower-income groups exhibited a tendency to fall. For instance, in the Philippines the bottom two deciles suffered a decline in real income in the period 1956–7 to 1970–1, whereas in Bangladesh during 1963–4 to 1975 the bottom eight deciles suffered such a decline. An independent study of Java indicates that during the period 1963–4 to 1969–70, in both rural and urban areas, there was a 'deterioration in real level of living for approximately the bottom 40 % of the population.'[4]

Third, in a few cases it was possible to do what ideally we would have liked to do in all cases, namely, examine changes in the living standards of relatively homogeneous occupational groups or classes, such as rubber smallholders in Malaysia, plantation workers in Sri Lanka or landless labourers in the Philippines. Where the data permitted we tried to convert nominal incomes into real incomes by deflating the former with class-specific price indexes. Our results indicate that throughout Asia the incomes of many smallholders and landless workers have fallen.

After completion of our research I undertook a cursory examination of the literature from elsewhere in order to determine whether the cases we studied were unique or unrepresentative. This literature is heterogeneous, using sources of data and methods different from our own, but the findings are often broadly consistent with ours. As a strategy of development, 'trickle down' has seldom worked satisfactorily. For example, evidence from areas of Asia not included in our studies suggests that the incomes of the poor probably have declined there too. For instance, even average income per head tended to fall during 1967–73 in Afghanistan and Nepal, and there is now a presumption that the poor did even less well than the average. Data from parts of India not included in our studies indicate that real wage rates of male field labourers have fallen significantly in the decade beginning in 1961–2 in Assam, Karnataka, Madhya Pradesh, Orissa, Maharashtra and West Bengal, and in all these states except Madhya Pradesh real wages were higher in 1956–7 than in 1971–2.[5]

The data become more scarce and less reliable when one turns to Africa. Nevertheless it is apparent that poverty is increasing in many parts of that continent. Indeed, average incomes fell between 1960 and 1973 in at least half a dozen states, namely, Chad, Niger, Senegal, Somalia, Sudan and Upper Volta.[6] Guinea and Ghana experienced total stagnation of *per capita* income and there is no doubt that in both countries the position of the poor deteriorated. In fact the real income of cocoa producers in Ghana was 23 per cent lower in 1969 than it was in 1958.[7]

It would be a mistake, however, to attribute the rise in poverty to slow aggregate rates of growth. Even in countries where average incomes are thought to have increased, e.g. in Ethiopia, Zaire and Zambia, it is probable that those of the poor declined. In Tanzania between 1969 and 1975 the real incomes of the urban poor, i.e. those in the informal sector, fell by about a half and the incomes of smallholder farmers in the poorest regions fell by about 17 per cent.[8]

In North Africa, the bottom 40 per cent of rural households and the bottom 20 per cent of urban households in Morocco experienced a fall in real consumption between 1959–60 and 1970–1.[9] In Egypt, real wages in agriculture have fluctuated around a zero trend from 1938 to 1974. They reached a peak in 1951, fell to their lowest point in 1955, then rose to their highest point in 1966. Since then they have fallen steadily, so that by 1974 real wages were 26 per cent lower than in 1966. Landless families accounted for 60.6 per cent of agricultural families in 1950. After the land reforms the proportion fell to 45.3 per cent in 1961 but rose thereafter to 50 per cent in 1972. Thus in the last decade or so in rural Egypt real wages have been falling and the proportion of households dependent on wages for a livelihood has been rising.[10] The urban poor of Egypt have probably suffered in a similar manner and this suffering is the likely underlying cause of the riots in Cairo and other cities of the Nile Valley in January 1977.

In Latin America, too, there is a suspicion that considerable numbers of people have failed to benefit from the growth that undoubtedly occurred in the last two or three decades. Haiti and Uruguay have experienced many years of economic decline, but most of the other countries in the Western Hemisphere have enjoyed a substantial rise in average income per head. Yet poverty persists and may have become accentuated in certain regions and for certain social classes.

A study of Mexico, for example, indicates that the share of the bottom 40 per cent has fallen dramatically since 1950. Moreover, the real income of this group appears to have increased by at most 9 per cent between 1950 and 1968–9.[11] Over a longer period it appears that 'the material lot of the poorest 40 per cent of Mexican families has changed negligibly since 1910.'[12] It is possible that if one were able to disaggregate and regroup the data into homogenous occupational categories one would find that the standard of living of many Mexican workers actually had fallen. Work done by myself in the neighbouring country of Guatemala in the late 1960s indicates that 'the income and consumption of the poorest members of society have been falling'.[13] More recent work on Central America, concentrating on the period 1960–71, reports that 'annual real earnings . . . appear to be falling for many landless rural workers in the most labor-abundant regions of El Salvador and Guatemala, while only increased participation of women and children in wage labor permits family incomes to be maintained.'[14]

A careful analysis of income distribution in Colombia indicates that the 'pure labor share' has fallen from 66–84 per cent of agricultural value added in 1935–9 to 35–43 per cent in 1960–4.[15] Furthermore, in the rural areas, 'real daily wage rates appear to have been about the same in the latter part of the 1960s as they were in the mid-1930s.'[16] After suitable qualifications the authors conclude that 'a non-increasing wage rate probably indicates a non-increasing or very slowly increasing real income for a majority of the labor force.'[17] This view is supported by direct evidence from three small-farm communities in Colombia which indicates that the standard of living of some groups of the poor possibly has even deteriorated.[18] Between 1963 and 1970 the fall in *per capita* income in the three communities was about 31 per cent.[19] This was accompanied by a fall in the quantity of meat consumed per family in two out of three communities, and by a fall in real expenditure on food, clothing and medicines in all three communities.

Indirect evidence from Ecuador suggests that since the early 1960s 'there was a sustained but gradual deterioration in the standard of living of the *campesino* population inhabiting the Sierra.'[20] In Peru the available data indicate that 'most of the rural population, particularly that of the Sierra, and some groups of self-employed workers such as artisans and domestics, have become relatively poorer over the period' 1950 to 1966.[21] The author of the study, Richard Webb, while emphasising that his conclusions are highly tentative, none the less suggests 'that for a large proportion of the population, which could plausibly range between 15% to 25%, there has been no absolute improvement in living standards.'[22] This group consists largely of small farmers with 5 hectares or less.

Thus the readily available material from Mexico, Central America and Western South America, although incomplete and of varying reliability, is broadly consistent. Significant groups of the rural population, notably small farmers and landless workers, either have experienced no increase in their material well-being or have suffered some decline. Indeed, the United Nations Economic Commission for

Latin America estimates that between 1960 and 1970 the share in income of the poorest 20 per cent of the population in Latin America declined from 3.1 to 2.5 per cent and the *per capita* income of this group rose by only $2 (in 1960 prices).[23] Given that broadly similar phenomena can be observed throughout the Third World—an increasing number and often an increasing proportion of impoverished people even in countries which have experienced growth of output per head—it is natural that one should begin to search for elements which these countries have in common which could account for their similar performance.

I. ELEMENTS OF AN EXPLANATION

The increase in poverty that we have detected is concentrated in rural areas. This growing poverty, however, has relatively little to do with rates of growth of aggregate production, although in the few cases where output per head has fallen this obviously constitutes an important part of the explanation. Equally, the growing impoverishment in the Third World is not associated with sluggish sectoral growth rates or the failure to expand of specific groups of commodities such as food. World agricultural production per head has modestly but noticeably increased during the last two decades. The same is true of world food production per head. Indeed, only in Africa is it possible that food output may not have kept pace with population expansion. In general, however, 'there is little reason to anticipate severe food supply limitations in the medium-term future.'[24] Thus one is more likely to encounter the reasons for the persistence of poverty by examining not the rate of growth but the structure of the economy and the pattern of growth that structure generates.

One feature that is common to the majority of Third World countries is the high degree of inequality of income and wealth, particularly landed wealth. In many countries the bottom 20 per cent of households receive only 4 to 7 per cent of total income whereas the top 20 per cent receive nearly half or even more. This inequality results in a compression of the incomes of the poorest members of the population and the concentration of the potentially investible surplus in the hands of a small minority. In turn, the disposal of this surplus between consumption of the upper-income groups, arms expenditure, unproductive and productive investment determine the speed and composition of material expansion.

The economies with which we are primarily concerned, viz. those in which the phenomenon of increasing poverty has been observed, are essentially mixed capitalist economies in which some decisions are taken centrally by government and most in response to decentralised price signals. The government of such an economy typically is a guardian of the *status quo*: it reflects the interests of the propertied classes and those allied to them and adopts policies which on balance are designed to perpetuate the hegemony of those classes. In such an economy the sets of relative prices which guide consumption and production decisions are strongly affected: first, by the distribution of income and the underlying structure of asset ownership; second, by the resulting composition of demand; and third, by the ways in which government chooses to intervene in the functioning of the economy.

In the majority of countries factor markets are organised in such a way that inequalities arising from an unequal distribution of wealth are accentuated by the price system. Those who have access to the formal capital markets are able to obtain finance on very favourable terms, whereas those who must rely on the informal market pay a price for credit which is a multiple of that paid by the privileged few. Similar phenomena, *mutatis mutandis*, can be observed in the land and labour markets, in the markets and administrative arrangements through which foreign exchange is allocated, and in the bureaucratic procedures which are used to allocate services provided directly by the state. In consequence, most of the investible surplus is controlled by a minority of property owners who adopt mechanised techniques of production capable of providing employment for only a minority of the labour force. In contrast, the great majority of the labour force is compelled to seek a livelihood in low-productivity and low-income activities which, from a social cost-benefit point of view, are excessively labour-intensive. Rough calculations made by Frances Stewart, for example, indicate that if the underdeveloped countries adopt the techniques used in the 'average of developed countries', savings per head are sufficient to employ only about 0.3 per cent of the labour force in India, 6.2 per cent in Sri Lanka and 13.1 per cent in Brazil.[25] The rest of the labour force, presumably, would have to work without the benefit of capital.

Superimposed upon this socio-economic structure are four dynamic forces which tend to perpetuate and even aggravate the poverty of important groups in the rural areas.

First, there is private investment. The volume of such investment is low in proportion to the economic surplus appropriated by those who control the national wealth. Average gross savings are about 16 per cent,[26] and the net rate would be, say, approximately 12 per cent, with considerable variation around this average. Not all of this savings and investment originates in the private sector, of course, although much of it does.[27] Although some of the private investment is located in rural areas, 80 per cent of it or more is channelled into the urban areas, notwithstanding the fact that the urban population accounts for only 19 per cent of the total in Africa and South Asia, and even in Latin America 40 per cent of the population still lives in rural areas. This 'urban bias'[28] in the pattern of investment often takes the form of highly-mechanised projects in which the share of wages in value added is relatively low. As a result, the rate of employment creation in the capital-intensive sector is slow, sometimes not even as fast as the rate of growth of the labour force. This phenomenon is common in Latin America and Asia.

Those unable to obtain employment in the capital-intensive activities must seek a livelihood either in the urban informal sector or in rural areas, or become openly unemployed. If the labour force entering these categories expands faster than the rate of accumulation in the informal sector and rural areas combined, there is likely to be downward pressure on the real incomes of the most vulnerable workers in the most vulnerable sectors.

Second, these pressures are likely to be exacerbated by trends in state investment. The reason for this is that in mixed economies state investment is essentially supportive of private-sector enterprises, especially the large and capital-intensive enterprises. This, in turn, reflects the fact that the social forces on which the state depends for its support are the same social forces which own the wealth of the country, supply the technicians and administrators and provide the leadership of the army, the religious hierarchies and the dominant political groups. Economic and political influence are closely interwoven: those who possess purchasing power also possess political power.

The role of the government in perpetuating poverty and inequality is also reflected in its expenditure policies for social welfare, i.e. health, education, social security and public housing. Rarely are the programmes designed in such a way that the benefits received by the lowest-income groups are absolutely larger than the benefits received by those with above-average incomes. In fact, often the programmes are not even 'progressive', i.e. the distribution of benefits from government expenditures is even more unequal than the distribution of income. This can easily occur where the coverage of a government programme is relatively narrow and fails to reach many groups living in poverty.

Third, the process of technical innovation is likely to have a labour-saving bias in the activities in which most of the investment occurs. Part of the explanation for this is that the pattern of innovation is certain to be affected by the set of relative factor prices which large investors confront. We have already seen that these factor prices encourage the adoption of relatively mechanised techniques which economise on labour. Another part of the explanation is that the economies under study are dependent for much of their innovation on imported foreign technology.[29] This technology was developed in economies where labour is scarce and capital is abundant, and hence their importation into countries where the opposite conditions prevail is likely to diminish still further the amount of employment created per dollar of investment.

Thus in activities where most of the surplus is invested—in manufacturing, on the large mechanised farms, in port, airport and highway development—there is a danger that the process of innovation will be increasingly labour-displacing. In the rest of the economy, however, where most of the labour force is occupied, the investible surplus is small and producers are forced by circumstances to seek land- and capital-saving innovations. At times this process may be pushed so far that the ratio of labour to land and capital begins to rise and a process of increasing poverty, declining labour productivity and 'agricultural involution' is initiated.[30]

Whether and to what extent this happens depends, of course, upon our fourth dynamic process: demographic forces. Given the structure of the economy as we have described it and the resulting nature of the processes of accumulation and innovation, the faster the rates of growth of the population and labour force, the stronger will be the tendency for the standard of living of some groups or classes to fall. Unfortunately, with few exceptions, rough estimates of the present rates of demographic expansion in the Third World indicate that population growth rates, while beginning to fall, remain high.

As was emphasised on page 131, however, the cause of increasing poverty is not rapid population growth. This is merely a contributing factor. The basic causes are the unequal ownership of land and other productive assets, allocative mechanisms which discriminate in favour of the owners of wealth, and a pattern of investment and technical change which is biased against labour.

Because of the rate and pattern of accumulation and innovation, the amount of labour that can be readily absorbed in urban areas and in non-farm rural activities is relatively small—far smaller than the increase in the labour force. Agricultural production is characterised by diminishing returns to labour, which of course in principle could be offset by high rates of investment and technical change. Unfortunately, however, investment in agriculture has been modest, especially on the small farms, yet the sector has been forced to retain a large fraction of the annual increase in the labour force.

As a result, the tendency toward diminishing returns and falling labour productivity has not always been compensated by rising investment. As the land – man ratio has fallen, the level and share of rents has increased while the wage share, wage rates and the number of days employed per person have tended to fall. That is, at the going terms of agricultural remuneration, the demand for labour has increased less rapidly than the supply, and hence the standard of living has fallen of those who depend on work as a source of income. This has affected some plantation workers, unskilled landless agricultural labourers, pure tenants and some small landowners who have to supplement their income by engaging in paid labour.

Thus it is that in a world that is far from being perfectly competitive, a rise in national income per head and in food production per head is quite compatible, not only with greater relative inequality, but with greater hunger and falling incomes for the poorest members of society.

II. TOWARDS AN ALTERNATIVE DEVELOPMENT STRATEGY

We have concentrated on the fact of impoverishment and its causes. Let us now turn to the normative aspects of poverty, in which value judgements inevitably intermingle with positive analysis in suggesting remedies. Indeed, in some sense, the idea of poverty is itself subjective.

The well-being of an individual, household or collectivity depends on many things—the level of money income and of prices, the volume of production for self-consumption, the distribution of purchasing power, the allocation of government expenditure, the extent of participation in making the important decisions which affect one's life, and the related question of the extent to which society is divided into classes and the degree of social mobility. Well-being, in other words, is a multi-dimensional concept; it depends in part on the absolute level of real income and consumption, in part on the relative distribution of income, wealth, power and social status, and in part on the ease with which it is possible to move from one occupation or social category to another. To express it in yet another way, the notion of well-being contains both stock and flow elements, both absolute and relative dimensions, and both static and dynamic characteristics.

It has long been recognised that the notion of well-being is too complex to be reduced to a single index number. Thomas Carlyle, for example, writing his *Chartism* in 1839, asked 'What constitutes the well-being of a man?' In part, he said, it is wages and the amount of bread his wages will buy, but he then added that man does not live by bread alone.

Can the labourer, by thrift and industry, hope to rise to mastership; or is such hope cut off from him? How is he related to his employer—by bonds of friendliness and mutual help, or by hostility, opposition and chains of mutual necessity alone? . . . With hunger preying on him, his contentment is likely to be small! But even with abundance, his discontent, his real misery may be great. The labourer's feelings, his notion of being justly dealt with or unjustly; his wholesome composure, frugality, prosperity in the one case, his acrid unrest, recklessness, gin-drinking and gradual ruin in the other—how shall figures of arithmetic represent all this?

The answer, of course, is that they can't and it would be idle to pretend that the 'figures of arithmetic' we have cited do more than illuminate a small part of the problem of the lack of well-being of much of mankind. None the less, by assuming everything else is equal, it has often been argued that a rise in national income *per capita* (for the nation) or in disposable income (for the family) is indicative of an increase in welfare and a decline in poverty. League tables of GNP *per capita* and rates of growth of GNP have been widely used to assess the extent of international poverty and the rate at which welfare is rising. Within nations, 'poverty lines' have been drawn, as was done in some of the studies mentioned earlier, with the implication, presumably, that poverty will have been eliminated once those below the line are able to rise above it.

Increasingly, however, it has become accepted that *per capita* income is an inadequate measure of well-being and that poverty is not an absolute concept that can be delineated by a poverty line. A family just below the poverty line in the United States obviously would not be considered poor in Nigeria, for example. Similarly, a household in England earning £70 a week in 1977 would be well above the poverty line, whereas an identical household with the same real income in 1997 might be considered rather poor. The point of these simple illustrations is that one's well-being or prosperity is relative; it is intimately related to the standard of living of one's neighbours.

Once this point is fully accepted, the idea that some items are absolute necessities, or that poverty is inversely related to income, must be abandoned. This was clear to Adam Smith two centuries ago when he stated that 'By necessities I understand not only the commodities which are indispensably necessary for the support of life, but whatever the custom of the country renders it indecent for creditable people, even of the lowest order, to be without.'[31] If 'custom' determines 'necessities', and if poverty is defined in relative terms, then it will not be possible to reduce poverty and increase well-being merely by raising the average level of income.

It has already been shown that it is possible for the incomes of the poorest groups to decline absolutely while the average for the nation rises. The point that is now being made, however, goes beyond this. That is, our view of poverty as a relative concept implies that the solution to the problem consists not so much in raising average income as in reducing dispersion around the average. Similarly, if one wishes to determine whether or not poverty has diminished one should first try to find out whether inequality has declined, and then whether income per head has risen.[32] China, for example, has succeeded in reducing poverty dramatically, not by achieving extraordinarily rapid rates of growth, but by achieving an unusual degree of equality. The symptom of well-being in China, or the absence of glaring poverty, is the uniformity of standards of consumption, not the high average level of consumption.

In the countries with which we are concerned, most of the poverty is in the rural areas and in most rural areas poverty is intimately related to the degree of land concentration. A reduction in the inequality of land-ownership through a redistribution of property in favour of landless workers, tenants and small farmers would contribute directly to the alleviation of the most acute forms of poverty. Moreover, a redistribution of land through the creation of smallholdings is likely to reduce poverty indirectly by increasing production and total income.

The reason for this is that small farmers typically use production technologies, cropping patterns and rotation systems which are more productive than those used by large farmers. Specifically, small farmers tend to cultivate any given crop with more labour-intensive techniques. They also tend to choose a composition of crop and livestock activities which is more labour-intensive. Finally, small farmers tend to use their land more intensively: one typically finds that, as the size of farm increases, the proportion of the land which is uncultivated, in fallow or in natural pastures also increases.

As a result, employment per hectare rises, and output per worker falls, as the average size of farm declines. Similarly, yields and value added per hectare rise as the average size of farm declines. These tendencies have been observed throughout the world, including several countries in Latin America.

The inverse relationship between farm size and output per hectare is in fact well established. Moreover, the evidence indicates that the relationship cannot be attributed to differences in land quality, soil fertility or the presence of irrigation. The differences in employment and output per hectare are due to differences in the behaviour of farmers, not to environmental differences. Even on a crop-by-crop basis, it appears that yields decline as farm size increases. The relationship is reinforced, however, by changes in the output mix.

It is increasingly becoming accepted that the explanation for the inverse relationship lies in the systematic difference in relative factor prices which small and large farmers confront.[33] Interest rates on borrowed capital and the rental price of land are usually higher for the smaller farmers, while the wage rates for labour are sometimes higher for the larger farmer. As a result, the incentive system induces farmers to shift towards relatively higher land/labour and capital/labour ratios as the size of farm increases. These tendencies are often accentuated by public sector agencies which channel their services (technical assistance, credit, etc.) disproportionately toward the larger farmers.

The larger farmers, in consequence, often appear to be more innovative or 'progressive'. Indeed studies of the 'green revolution' have shown that the larger farmers were usually the first to introduce the new seed-fertiliser technology. Despite the adoption of high-yielding varieties however, value added per hectare continues to be less on the large farms than on the small; the high degree of labour intensity on the small farms more than compensates for the higher degree of capital intensity on the large.

It is important not to romanticise about the peasantry or exaggerate their comparatively higher total factor productivity. The intensity with which small farmers cultivate their land is a reflection not of their moral worth but of the severe scarcity of resources complementary to their labour. In a sense, much of the peasantry is forced to engage in self-exploitation on small holdings because this is the only means of survival. Be that as it may, it follows from our analysis that a redistribution of land to small cultivators would increase both employment and output.

A reduction in inequality, therefore, if brought about through a redistribution of landed property and supported by subsidiary measures such as the provision of credit and marketing facilities, is likely to raise total production and certainly will raise the incomes of the poor. Under some circumstances it may also lead to an increase in the rate of growth of production. Dynamic processes affecting the rate of growth, however, are rather unpredictable and their discussion necessarily remains somewhat speculative.

Much depends upon the historical circumstances which produced the land reform and the redistribution of income. Indeed, land reforms are sometimes introduced by those who have an interest in preserving the *status quo* and in stabilising a social and political system. That is, paradoxically, they have been introduced as part of a programme to maintain maximum feasible inequality. In these cases the effects of the redistributive measures are minimal. On the other hand, where redistributive measures have been introduced as a direct result of massive pressure from the peasantry, land reforms have tended to initiate a process of cumulative development and a sustained reduction in poverty. Indeed, it has been rightly stated that 'rural development cannot be said to have begun without land reform.'[34] Thus the participation of the peasantry is essential, first, in order to ensure that a substantial initial redistribution occurs and, second, to ensure that land redistribution becomes not just an end in itself but a stimulus to further progress.[35] It is becoming more and more widely recognised that rural development, to be successful, must be not only for the people but also by them.

Because of differences in historical circumstances and in the extent of participation by the poor, it is impossible to generalise about the effects of redistribution on growth. Most observers now believe, however, that 'it is difficult to identify clear evidence of a trade-off between growth, however defined or measured, and distribution.'[36] Moreover, a consensus may be emerging gradually that the only way effectively to redistribute income is to redistribute wealth. An analysis of the historical experience of South Korea, Taiwan, Sri Lanka, Cuba and Tanzania has led some observers to conclude that 'in all cases, successful redistribution seems to have been preceded or accompanied by changes in the structure of asset ownership, particularly by land reform.'[37]

Our own conclusions are as follows. First, it is desirable and necessary that the mass of the population actively participate in the formulation and implementation of policies to reduce poverty. Second, a redistribution of productive assets, notably land, is likely to be an essential component of any development strategy designed to improve the living standards of the very poor and to reduce inequality. Third, land reform is likely to result not only in greater equality but also in higher output; furthermore, there is no reason to believe that it will reduce the rate of growth of agricultural output, and it may increase it.

Undoubtedly the key to greater prosperity for the poor is a combination of greater equality and faster growth. This was well illustrated in a recent report prepared by the International Labour Organisation,[38] of which the present writer was one of the authors.

In that report minimum consumption objectives—basic needs—were established for food, housing, education and, implicitly, for health. These specific items were used as a proxy for the larger basket of basic needs and this basket, in turn, was converted into an income equivalent by estimating from household expenditure data the level of income necessary to satisfy the household's basic needs. It was assumed that the objective is to meet the basic needs of the poorest 20 per cent of the population, most of whom are in rural areas, within one generation. This target implies that by the year 2000 all households except those with an income below the average of the lowest quintile would have met their basic needs. It was further assumed, optimistically perhaps, that the population would follow the United Nation's low growth rate projection, implying a rapid fall in the rate of demographic expansion.

Calculations were first made of the rate of growth that would be necessary until the year 2000 to achieve the basic needs target, assuming no redistribution occurred. In the case of China the required rate of growth turned out to be 6.0 per cent per annum. Given that China grew 6.3 per cent a year between 1965 and 1973 such a strategy for achieving basic needs is feasible. In the case of the other medium- and low-income countries of Asia, however, the required rate of growth was much higher, namely 9.7 per cent a year and in Latin America the required growth rate was between 8.7 and 9.4 per cent a year. The required growth rates in Africa were much higher still. Since the recent rate of growth of these countries is much lower than this it is unrealistic to hope that growth alone will enable the poor to attain their basic needs. Indeed, as we have seen, the modest growth that has been achieved so far has resulted in many of the very poor becoming absolutely poorer. Clearly some redistributive measures are necessary.

Next, assuming countries were able to grow 6 per cent per annum for a generation, the growth rate being that of the International Strategy adopted by the United Nations for the Second Development Decade, calculations were made of the amount of redistribution that would be necessary to achieve the basic needs targets. Specifically, estimates were made of what the share of the poorest 20 per cent of households would have to become by the year 2000 in order to meet the objectives. In the case of China, the share of the poorest quintile already is well over 10 per cent and, as is apparent from the previous paragraph, no further redistribution is necessary. In the case of the other medium- and low-income countries of Asia, however, the basic needs of the population could be met only if 6 per cent growth were combined with a radical redistribution of income such that the share of the poorest quintile rose from 5.3 per cent at present to 14.3 per cent. That is, the share of the poor would have to increase nearly three times and the degree of equality would have to exceed that of China. Evidently such a strategy is not feasible.

A broadly similar picture emerged for Africa and Latin America. In arid Africa the share of the bottom quintile would have to rise to 12.4 per cent, and in tropical Africa to 16.5 per cent! In Latin America the rise would have to be from about 4.4 per cent to between 11.3 and 11.9 per cent. Clearly such a strategy is not feasible in Africa and Latin America either.

Finally, the rate of growth that would be required to satisfy basic needs within the stipulated time was recalculated on the assumption that income was redistributed until it became as equal as the ILO believed it to be in China, i.e. until the share of the poorest 20 per cent reached 11.3 per cent. Under this assumption, in order for the Third World to meet the basic needs objective within a generation, an annual rate of growth of 7.2 per cent is needed in the medium- and low-income countries of Asia, 8.4 to 8.8 per cent in Africa and about 6.7 per cent in Latin America.

The model on which the growth calculations are based did not require one to distinguish between an initial, once-for-all redistribution and a series of annual incremental redistributions; all that was specified in the model is the distribution of income at the end of the period, i.e. the year 2000. In applying the insights of the model in practice, however, a large initial redistribution would be preferred, since the sooner redistribution occurs the higher will be the standard of living of the poor in the intervening years between the initiation of a basic needs strategy and its completion.

Moreover, the model was concerned with the distribution of income and is silent about the distribution of wealth. In practice, however, measures which attempt to redistribute income without affecting the distribution of wealth are likely to be impossible. This is partly because it is difficult to confine the effects of standard price, subsidy, tax and expenditure policies to a particular group and partly because the effects of many standard economic policies ultimately are neutralised by offsetting forces set in motion by the policies themselves.[39] For example, the benefits of a rural road-building programme cannot be limited to small farmers; they inevitably 'spill over' or 'leak' to large farmers as well. Similarly, the imposition of a minimum wage for landless agricultural labourers will have multifarious implications for, say, the costs of agricultural production, the demand for labour, the level of food prices and of prices in general—all of which will tend to counteract the effects of the legislation on the distribution of income. Thus because of leakages and countervailing forces the only way to alter substantially the distribution of income is by altering the distribution of wealth. In agricultural countries this implies above all the need for land reform.

It is obvious that the objectives of most Third World governments are inconsistent with the policies implicit in a basic needs strategy, namely, a sharp acceleration in the rate of growth combined with a radical redistribution of income and wealth. The strategy itself, however, is feasible; it is capable of being implemented. Indeed, it has been successfully implemented on a gigantic scale in a country that only a generation ago suffered from appalling poverty, China. Logic and experience have shown that within a remarkably short period a people can construct by their own efforts, unaided, a new society in which no one goes hungry or without adequate shelter, clothing and communal facilities. Poverty, then, is a product of particular societies and it can be eradicated only by changing those societies.

NOTES AND REFERENCES

1. ILO, *Poverty and Landlessness in Rural Asia* (1977).
2. It was not possible to construct a poverty line in Sri Lanka and Indonesia.
3. One exception was Tamil Nadu, India where the proportion below the poverty line fell from 74.1% in 1957–8 to 64.4% in 1963–4 and then rose again to 74% in 1969–70. The other exception was Pakistan, which exhibited a similar pattern. For a summary of the eight studies see Ch. 6.
4. Dwight Y. King and Peter D. Weldon, 'Income Distribution and Levels of Living in Java, 1963–1970', *Economic Development and Cultural Change* (July 1977) p. 710.
5. *Poverty, Unemployment and Development Policy: A Case Study of Selected Issues with Reference to Kerala*, Centre for Development Studies, Trivandrum (Mar. 1975) Vol. I, Table 8.3, p. viii–4.
6. *World Bank Atlas* (1975).
7. ILO, *Les Revenus des Travailleurs Agricoles en Afrique Centrale et Occidentale*, Table 7, p. 50 (Geneva, 1975).
8. These are preliminary figures from a study being conducted by Paul Collier.
9. Keith Griffin, *Land Concentration and Rural Poverty* (London: Macmillan, 1976) Ch. 2, p. 75.
10. The data on Egypt were kindly supplied by Samir Radwan.

11. David Felix, 'Trickling Down in Mexico and the Debate over Long Term Growth-Equity Relationships in the LDCs', mimeo (1974) p. 16.

12. David Felix, 'Economic Growth and Income Distribution in Mexico', mimeo, p. 2 (forthcoming in *Current History*).

13. Keith Griffin, op. cit., Ch. 4, p. 164.

14. Clark Reynolds, 'Fissures in the Volcano?: Central American Economic Prospects', draft (Nov. 1976) p. 15.

15. Albert Berry and Miguel Urrutia, *Income Distribution in Colombia* (Yale University Press, 1976) Table 3.7, p. 68.

16. Ibid., p. 65.

17. Ibid., p. 69.

18. Robert L. Whittenbarger and A. Eugene Havens, 'A Longitudinal Analysis of Three Small-Farm Communities in Colombia: A Compendium of Descriptive Statistics', mimeo, Land Tenure Center, University of Wisconsin, LTC No. 87 (June 1973) Tables 5, 7, 11, 12 and 25.

19. This figure was obtained by deflating income in current prices with the cost of living index for Bogotá, the only consumer price index available.

20. Keith Griffin, op. cit., Ch. 5, p. 177.

21. Richard Webb, *Government Policy and the Distribution of Income in Peru, 1963–1973* (Harvard University Press, 1977) p. 38.

22. Ibid., p. 42.

23. Anibal Pinto, 'Styles of Development in Latin America', *CEPAL Review* (First Semester 1976) Table 7, p. 118.

24. Lance Taylor, 'The Misconstrued Crisis: Lester Brown and World Food', *World Development* (Nov./Dec. 1975) p. 832.

25. Frances Stewart, *Technology and Underdevelopment* (London: Macmillan, 1977) Table 3.9, p. 72.

26. See UN, *World Economic Survey, 1969–1970* (New York, 1971).

27. A recent study of seven underdeveloped countries indicates that gross private savings account on average for about 9.3 per cent of GNP. See Paul Jonas and Anjum Nasim, 'Public and Private Savings of Selected Developing Countries in the First UN Development Decade', *Pakistan Development Review* (Winter 1976) Table 2, p. 455.

28. Michael Lipton, *Why Poor People Stay Poor: Urban Bias in World Development* (London: Maurice Temple Smith, 1977).

29. In the early 1970s imported capital goods as a percentage of gross fixed investment were 63 per cent in Malaysia, 58 per cent in Indonesia, 43 per cent in the Philippines and 27–28 per cent in Pakistan and Sri Lanka; in India, in contrast, they were only 7 per cent. (See Frances Stewart, op. cit., Table 5.2, p. 121).

30. Clifford Geertz, *Agricultural Involution: The Process of Ecological Change in Indonesia* (University of California Press, 1968).

31. *The Wealth of Nations*, Book 5, Ch. 2, Part II.

32. A similar point of view has been expressed by Dudley Seers, 'The Meaning of Development', *International Development Review*, (1969) Vol. II, No. 4.

33. See, for example, Albert Berry and William R. Cline, *Farm Size, Factor Productivity and Technical Change in Developing Countries*, Draft (1976) and Keith Griffin, *The Political Economy of Agrarian Change* (London: Macmillan, 1974).

34. Wahidul Haque, Niranjan Mehta, Anisur Rahman and Ponna Wignaraja, *Towards a Theory of Rural Development*, (UN, Asian Development Institute, 1975) p. 96.
35. The importance of participation by the beneficiaries of reform is stressed by Joost B. W. Kuitenbrouwer, *Premises and Implications of a Unified Approach to Development Analysis and Planning* (UN, ESCAP, SD/SP/Ex In-3, 1975).
36. Hollis Chenery *et al.*, *Redistribution with Growth*, (London: Oxford University Press, 1974) p. 255.
37. Ibid.
38. *Employment, Growth and Basic Needs* (Geneva, ILO, 1976) Ch. 2.
39. See the Introduction to Keith Griffin, *Land Concentration and Rural Poverty*.

8. Inequality, effective demand and the causes of world hunger

Households become hungry and malnourished when the volume of resources they possess or can acquire (including labour power) and the terms on which they can be transformed into food become so unfavourable that an adequate diet can no longer be obtained. There are several reasons why this can occur.

First, the household may suffer a loss of resources. For example, the fertility of the land could be destroyed or impaired as a result, say, of erosion or increased salinity; or the labour services of the primary bread-winner could be lost through illness or death. In a dynamic context, the resources available to the household could decline if population growth were to proceed faster than the combined effects of the rate of accumulation of capital, the expansion of the cultivated area and the pace of resource-augmenting technical change.

Secondly, the resources available to the household may become less fully utilised. This is most likely to happen in the case of labour. Unemployment may be created as a consequence of a fall in aggregate demand (e.g. a reduction in the demand for investment goods or exports) or of a fall in the demand for specific types of labour (e.g. a reduction in the demand for harvest labour when poor crops are anticipated). In addition to these cyclical phenomena, there may be a secular tendency in some circumstances for the degree of underemployment to rise, as reflected for example in a gradual fall in the average number of days worked per year by agricultural labourers.

Third, even if a household's resources and their degree of utilisation remained unchanged, hunger may still arise because of an unfavourable change in the rate at which labour and marketable commodities can be exchanged for food. This could occur for a wide variety of reasons. For instance, the ratio of food prices to wages could rise as a result of a fall in the money wage rate. For example, the nominal wages of ploughmen in the Philippines fell between 1957 and 1961 and again between 1963 and 1965; money wages also fell in Bihar and eastern Uttar Pradesh, India, from about 1956 to 1961 and in Bangladesh from 1949 to 1955. Wages are not 'sticky' downwards in the rural areas of underdeveloped countries. Alternatively, the ratio of food prices to non-food prices could rise as a result, say, of a fall in the world price of rubber, as happened in Malaysia between 1959 and 1971. In the absence of technical change which raised output of rubber per hectare this evidently would reduce the standard of living of rubber producers and in the case of some smallholders could push their real income to the point of starvation.

Similarly, as in South Asia, food prices could rise. There might be a sudden fall in food supplies, perhaps as a consequence of natural or man-made catastrophes such as flood, droughts or wars. In the longer run the operation of diminishing returns to labour could lead to a rising marginal cost of food and hence to higher food prices. Equally, however, higher food prices could be caused primarily by growing demand, for example in the world market or among the more prosperous classes in the domestic market. Of course a rise in the relative price of food does not necessarily indicate that real incomes have fallen, let alone that hunger has increased, but in the conditions prevailing in many underdeveloped countries an adverse change in what Amartya Sen calls 'exchange entitlements'[1] is likely to be a prominent cause of growing hunger and malnutrition.

The conventional explanation of hunger focuses on the supply of food. Famines are usually attributed to a sudden decline in domestic production or in net imports, while chronic malnutrition is attributed to a failure of food production to keep up with population growth. Difficulties on the supply side clearly can be major causes of widespread hunger. Indeed, even a minor decline in the availability of food can in some circumstances result in starvation. Where this occurs, however, the reason is less likely to be that the average availability of food barely covers the subsistence needs of the population as that the distribution of the available food is highly unequal.

A prominent characteristic of the underdeveloped countries is that the poor spend most of their income on food, but a disproportionate amount of the food is consumed by the rich. It is well known from household sample surveys that the lower-income groups spend a very high proportion of their income on food. Thus in India, for example, food accounts for two-thirds to four-fifths of total expenditure by households with below-average incomes.[2] Yet even in relatively more developed regions of the Third World such as Latin America, the poor account for a small proportion of total food consumption. The United Nations Economic Commision for Latin America estimates that the poorest 20 per cent of the population consumed only 5 per cent of the value of all food, beverages and tobacco whereas the richest 10 per cent accounted for 29 per cent of consumption; even in the case of cereals, the poorest 20 per cent accounted for 8 per cent while the top 10 per cent accounted for 19 per cent.[3] Of course, it is the distribution of calories (and proteins) which matters most, not the distribution of the value of output, but it is clear that, however it is measured, the distribution of food is unequal.

This characteristic of the market for food in underdeveloped countries can be incorporated into an analysis of hunger by assuming that households can be divided roughly into two classes, the poor and the rich. There is a demand curve for food corresponding to each class, the difference in which primarily is due to the marked difference in average income per household in each class. These two demand curves are drawn in Figure 8. The demand curves are drawn as straight lines merely to facilitate the exposition. In practice, of course, they are likely to be non-linear. For example, if all the income of the poor were spent on food, an extreme assumption, their demand schedule over the relevant range would be a rectangular hyperbola and have an elasticity of unity.

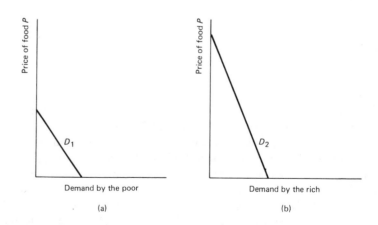

FIGURE 8

The aggregate demand curve for food D_3 is simply the horizontal summation of the two class demand curves, that of the poor D_1 and the rich D_2. This curve is drawn in Figure 9. Note that the aggregate curve is kinked at the point where the price of food reaches a height at which the poor are driven from the market.[4]

If initially the marketed supply of food in Figure 9 is S_1 and demand is D_3, the market price will tend to be P_1. A small reduction in supply may result in a sharp rise in price and, more important, may squeeze the real income of the poor to such an extent that they are forced to reduce their consumption of food and accept the consequential hunger. A fall in supply to S_2, for instance, would raise price to P_2, choke off all demand from the poor, and produce mass starvation.[5]

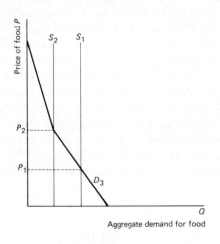

Aggregate demand for food

FIGURE 9

In practice, of course, the situation almost certainly will be more complex than this simple Marshallian analysis suggests. For example, a smaller harvest than usual will be associated with a lower demand for harvest labour, and the resulting lower wage rates and higher unemployment will be reflected in a downward shift of D_1 and that portion of D_3 below the kink. These effects on wage rates and employment sometimes associated with rises in food prices could become significant for the poor and, if so, they would lead to a shift of the lower portion of the food demand curve. Similarly, several qualifications could be added to the supply side of the analysis, notably the introduction of a positive supply elasticity of marketed production and a discussion of the effects on total availabilities of changes in foreign trade in food and in food stocks.

The simple Marshallian analysis, however, captures the essence of the argument of those who claim that famines are caused by reductions in supply. But the analysis also underlines the fact that famines are not a problem of supply only. In periods of shortage some people go hungry and others do not and it would be naive to believe that the probability of starvation after a bad harvest is the same for everyone. Death from hunger is not random. Who goes hungry, or starves, and how many, depends largely upon the way in which purchasing power (and hence income and wealth) are distributed. In an inegalitarian society in which a minority of the population accounts for a majority of food purchases, a small proportionate change in supply can cause a large proportion of the population to experience hunger, whereas a similar fall in production in a more egalitarian society may have no adverse effects on nutrition. Thus even in an analysis in which the availability of food is emphasised, the distribution of the effective demand for food must not be ignored.

Moreover, it is possible for famines to occur even when the supply of food remains unchanged. In at least some cases, famine conditions may originate not from a reduction in supply but from a rise in food prices following an increase in the demand for food. Of course, if the increased demand for food were uniform across all classes, the distribution of food among households would remain unaltered. On the other hand, if food prices rose as a result of increased demand from one section of the community only, the higher prices could squeeze some consumers out of the market.

There are several reasons why the increased demand might be concentrated among a small proportion of those who normally participate in the market. For example, there might be a sudden spurt of export demand. Or political events could provoke traders to purchase and hoard food in substantial quantities for speculative purposes. Or the rise in demand could be due to the fact that some groups experience a windfall rise in incomes while others do not. Whatever the reason, a rise in demand that is confined to a particular segment of the market will be reflected in higher food prices and a consequent fall in the quantity demanded by those who are squeezed. If the increase in prices and reduction in volume of purchases are large, the adversely affected groups could suffer severely.[6]

Something like this appears to have happened in the great Bengal famine of 1943 in which perhaps three million people died. Amartya Sen reckons that there was no significant decline in the availability of food grains during the famine period, yet between December 1941 and May 1943 the price of rice increased 457 per cent while the daily wage rate of male, agricultural, unskilled labour rose only 35 per cent, i.e. the purchasing power of wages in terms of rice fell by about three-fourths.[7]

The causes of the rise in the ratio of food prices to agricultural wages are rather complicated—Sen mentions seven factors that were operating[8]—but it is clear that the main pressure was coming from the side of demand. Aggregate demand rose sharply in Bengal because of activities associated with the war effort and in particular 'military and civil construction at a totally unprecedented scale.' This demand and higher incomes, however, were concentrated among the urban population of Calcutta and thus the rural population were forced to bear the resulting inflation without participating in the accompanying rise in real incomes. In consequence, real incomes in rural areas actually fell, the terms on which labour could be transformed into food deteriorated dramatically, and mass starvation ensued.

The great Bengal famine is a graphic if extraordinary illustration of the thesis of this chapter, namely, that changes in the distribution of real income and hence of effective demand of the poor for food are the fundamental causes of hunger in underdeveloped countries. This thesis is depicted in Figure 10. Imagine as before that households are divided into the two classes of the poor and the rich. Assume that marketed food supplies S_1 and the demand of the poor D_1 remain constant while the income of the rich and hence their demand for food increases (so that D_2 in Figure 8(b) shifts to the right).

The effect of this, in Figure 10, is to increase the aggregate demand for food by displacing D_3 horizontally to the right to, say, D_4 in such a way that the point at which the demand curve becomes kinked remains at P_2. Figure 10 has been drawn so that the rise in demand of the rich pushes up the price of food from P_1 to P_2. As in Figure 9, this price increase is such that the poor become excluded from the market and starve, even though the availability of food has remained unchanged. It is in this manner that famines can be caused entirely by changes in demand.[9]

Famines are episodic, affecting relatively few people, but malnutrition is chronic and affects the majority of households in underdeveloped countries. Yet in none of the major regions of the world does the *per capita* daily consumption of calories fall short of the standard calories requirement by as much as 10 per cent. None the less it is estimated that in the mid-1960s about 56 per cent of the population of the Third World had a diet that failed to meet nutritional requirements

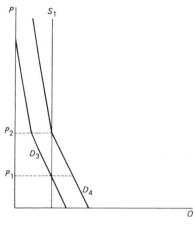

FIGURE 10

by more than 250 calories a day. Most of these people were in Asia and the numbers are growing.[10]

Food production in Asia, and in the Third World as a whole, has expanded at least as fast as the population. Indeed, between 1950 and 1973 gross agricultural output (of which food is by far the largest component) increased 3.8 per cent a year in the Third World while the annual rate of population growth was 2.4 per cent. The growth in income, furthermore, has been well in excess of demographic increase: the United Nations estimates that the GDP of the 'developing market

TABLE 11. Growth rates in Third World countries, 1950–1973 (per cent per annum)

	Population	Gross Agricultural Production	GDP per capita
Southern Europe	1.4	3.5	4.9
Middle East	3.0	3.3	5.6*
Africa	2.3	3.8	2.5*
South Asia	2.1	3.6	1.4*
East Asia	2.5	4.5	3.7
Western Hemisphere	2.8	3.4	2.5

* 1960–73

Source: Average growth rates calculated from data published in IBRD, *World Tables 1976* (Baltimore: Johns Hopkins University Press, 1976) Series III, Table 1.

economies' increased 5.6 per cent a year in the period 1960–75. Moreover, in each of the six regions of the Third World, as Table 11 indicates, average incomes increased significantly and agricultural production clearly out-paced population increase.

These are not conditions under which one would expect to encounter increased poverty and hunger. Yet a series of ten Asian case studies, in seven countries which between them account for 70 per cent of the rural population of the non-socialist Third World, indicates that there is some tendency in virtually every case for the proportion of the rural population in poverty to increase.[11] Moreover, since poverty almost always was defined with reference to some standard of nutritional adequacy, rising poverty is virtually synonymous with rising malnutrition.

A notable fact that arose from the studies is that 'there does not appear to be any clear relationship between the rate of increase in poverty and the rate of growth of the economy.'[12] For example, in Tamil Nadu, a slow-growing state of India, the proportion of the rural population in poverty was the same, viz. 74 per cent, in 1969–70 as in 1957–8, whereas in the rapidly-growing state of Uttar Pradesh, the proportion rose from 42 to 64 per cent in the decade ending in 1970–1.

Similarly, there is no simple association between changes in the incidence of rural poverty and the rate of growth of agricultural output per head. In Bangladesh, for example, *per capita* agricultural output has fallen and rural poverty has increased dramatically. In Sri Lanka, production and population have expanded at about the same rate, yet there has been some increase in poverty. In all other cases, there is a clear long-run tendency for agricultural output per head to rise,[13] yet the incidence of poverty has either remained roughly constant (e.g. in Pakistan) or has increased (e.g. Malaysia and the Philippines).

More important than the rate of growth is the pattern of growth.[14] In the cases examined it was found that the structure of the economy was typified by a high degree of inequality in the distribution of income and wealth, a class system which inhibited vertical social mobility and a fragmented price system which operated in such a way that the poor obtained scarce resources on less favourable terms than the rich. Associated with this social and economic structure were powerful dynamic forces which tend to perpetuate and even accentuate poverty and hunger.

One such force, or process occurring through time, is private investment, and its tendency to be concentrated in capital-intensive activities outside the rural areas. Another is the tendency for state investment to be essentially supportive of private sector enterprises, and thereby to reinforce the initial inequality. A third is the tendency for technical innovations to exhibit a labour-saving bias in the activities in which most of the investment occurs. This bias, in turn, is due in part to the signals transmitted by the fragmented price system and in part to the fact that much of the technology was developed in and imported from countries in which relative factor scarcities are the reverse of those prevailing in most of the Third World. Finally, these unequalising tendencies are exacerbated by rapid population growth.

The net effect of the interaction of these four dynamic processes with an inegalitarian economic structure is, often, to produce a combination of growth of average income per head and yet further impoverishment of the poor. This is reflected, in the rural areas, in a pattern of uneven development in which food supplies usually manage to keep up with the growth in population but tend to lag behind the growth in demand. [15] As a result, the relative price of food gradually rises. This squeezes the poor, forces them to reduce their consumption of food and thereby increases hunger and malnutrition. [16]

Income per head in the Philippines, for example, has increased about 2.5 per cent a year since the early 1960s and agricultural output per head increased 0.4 per cent a year during the period 1950–73, rising to 0.8 per cent a year from 1965 onwards. Yet a recent study indicates there has been a rising proportion of families with expenditures below the minimum amount required for nutritional adequacy as specified by the Food and Nutrition Research Center. In Greater Manila the proportion of families below this so-called food threshold rose from 17 per cent in 1965 to 25 per cent in 1971, and in rural areas over the same period the rise was from 39 to 48 per cent. The number of persons in families with expenditures below the threshold increased by 5 million during the period, while the total population increased 5.3 million, and the proportion of inadequately nourished people in the country rose from about 36.6 per cent to nearly 45 per cent. [17] This process of impoverishment was accompanied by rising relative food prices.

A dynamic version of the model in Figure 10 seems to be operative in many parts of the Third World. In these areas the problem of hunger cannot be overcome by accelerating aggregate growth while maintaining the existing pattern of growth. Indeed, in inegalitarian economies of the type we have described, for a given rate of growth of food production, the faster the growth of average income per head, the more does poverty increase. Moreover, as the experience of the so-called green revolution indicates, [18] it even is doubtful whether increasing food production would constitute by itself a solution.[19] The fundamental problem is not one of deficient supply but of insufficient purchasing power in the hands of the poor. This problem can be resolved, and world hunger eliminated, only through a massive redistribution of income and wealth, especially landed wealth. Measures short of this, such as increasing food output, while perhaps on balance beneficial, are essentially palliatives.

NOTES AND REFERENCES

1. Amartya Sen, 'Starvation and Exchange Entitlements: A General Approach and its Application to the Great Bengal Famine', *Cambridge Journal of Economics*, Vol. 1, No. 1 (Mar. 1977).
2. V. M. Dandekar and Nilakantha Rath, *Poverty in India* (Bombay: Economic and Political Weekly, 1971) Tables 1.2 and 1.3
3. Anibal Pinto, 'Styles of Development in Latin America', *CEPAL Review* (First Semester 1976) Table 4, p. 114.
4. The kinked demand curve arises from the fact that it is assumed that there are two homogeneous classes. If one assumes there are several more classes or a heterogeneous population without classes the demand curve would tend to become continuous in the usual way. The thrust of our argument, however, would not be affected by this alteration, although clarity of exposition would be sacrificed.
5. In fact, most deaths during famines are caused not by starvation but by ordinary illnesses to which the population has become more susceptible as a result of reduced consumption of food, by increased consumption of spoiled food, by greater exposure to the weather as the population moves about in search of food and by the associated decline in sanitary arrangements.
6. It might be thought that most households in underdeveloped countries consist of self-provisioning peasants and hence would be immune to the effects of a rise in the relative price of food. Unfortunately, this supposition is not correct. The majority consist of a diversity of classes which we have lumped together and called 'the poor', namely, landless labourers, plantation and forest workers, small landowners who supplement their income by engaging in off-farm activities, village artisans, transport workers and shopkeepers, fishermen and, of course, wage earners and the self-employed in urban areas. Thus, contrary to I. Adelman and S. Robinson in their book on *Income Distribution Policies in Developing Countries: A Case Study of Korea* (London: Oxford University Press, 1977), higher relative food prices are likely to result in greater poverty, not less.
7. Op. cit., Table 4, p. 44.
8. Ibid., section 6, pp. 49–51.
9. Some might argue that while food production may exhibit zero price elasticity, the elasticity of the marketed surplus will be positive. This undoubtedly is correct. It does not invalidate our argument, however, for unless the supply elasticity is infinite food prices will rise and under our assumptions this will tend to impoverish the poor.

10. Shlomo Reutlinger and Marcelo Selowsky, *Malnutrition and Poverty: Magnitude and Policy Options*, World Bank Staff Occasional Papers, No. 23 (1976).
11. The methodology employed in the ten studies as well as the results are summarised in Keith Griffin and Azizur Rahman Khan, 'Rural Poverty in Developing Countries: An Analysis of Trends with Special Reference to Contemporary Asia', paper prepared for the Fifth World Congress of the International Economic Association, Tokyo (26 Aug.–3 Sep. 1977).
12. Ibid., p. 4.
13. Growth Rates in Seven Asian Countries, 1950–73 (per cent per annum)

	Population	Gross Agricultural Production
Bangladesh*	2.8	1.7
India	2.1	2.8
Indonesia	2.1	3.2
Malaysia	2.9	3.9
Pakistan*	3.2	4.8
Philippines	3.0	3.4
Sri Lanka	2.5	2.4

Source: Average growth rates calculated from data published in IBRD, *World Tables 1976* (Baltimore: Johns Hopkins University Press, 1976) Series III, Table 1.

* 1960–1973

14. For an extended discussion see Ch. 6.
15. A recently published IBRD study has reached a similar conclusion, namely, that the long-term trend in underdeveloped countries is for food production to rise at least as fast as the population, but supply seems to be growing less rapidly than demand and hence there is a tendency for imports of food to increase or the prices of foodgrains to rise, or both. (See IBRD, *A Perspective on the Foodgrain Situation in the Poorest Countries*, World Bank Staff Working Paper No. 251 (Apr. 1977).
16. A broadly similar process was described by Kalecki as characteristic of 'intermediate regimes': 'The lagging of agriculture behind general economic growth leads to an inadequate supply of foodstuffs and an increase in their prices . . . . Even if the aggregate real incomes of those strata (i.e. the poor peasantry) do not decline . . . they do not show any appreciable growth.' (M. Kalecki, 'Observations on Social and Economic Aspects of "Intermediate Regimes"', *Essays on Developing Economies* (Hassocks: Harvester Press, 1976) p. 34.).
17. Mahar Mangahas and Raymunda Rimando, 'The Philippine Food Problem', mimeo (1976).
18. See Keith Griffin, *The Political Economy of Agrarian Change: An Essay on the Green Revolution* (London: Macmillan, 1974).

19. Even in the United States, the world's largest exporter of food, a significant amount of undernutrition persists among the poor while dietary illnesses caused by overeating are common among the rich.

9. Efficiency, equality and accumulation in rural China: notes on the Chinese system of incentives

One way of attempting to make an economic assessment of a system of socialist agriculture is to examine the efficiency with which resources are allocated, the degree to which equality is attained and the ability of the system to achieve a satisfactory rate of accumulation and technical change. These three aspects of overall economic performance ideally should not be seen in isolation since they obviously interact. For example, the pattern of resource allocation is inseparable from the pace of accumulation and both, in turn, affect the distribution of income. Be this as it may, however, I shall discuss the effects of the prevailing set of incentives in rural China under the headings of efficiency, equity and accumulation.

I. INCENTIVES AND EFFICIENCY

The problem of efficiency can be separated into two parts: the organisation of production and the composition of output. The first is concerned with the institutional arrangements under which production occurs and the second with the consequences of these arrangements for the level and pattern of production.

Efficient institutional arrangements should have at least four characteristics. First, they should help to ensure that all productive resources are fully utilised. Next, they should enable producers to take advantage of decreasing costs and economies of scale in those field operations, crops or services in which they arise while avoiding unnecessary costs associated with diseconomies of scale and cumbersome administrative procedures. Then, they should be sufficiently flexible to permit new factor combinations to emerge in response to changes in technology or in demand. Lastly, they should enable the rural community as a whole to spread (and hopefully to reduce) the risks of agricultural production.

How well do Chinese rural institutions perform by these criteria? In general the evidence presented to us by Unger[1] and others suggests that the performance is rather good. In particular, the Chinese have been remarkably successful in fully utilising their most abundant resource, labour. Indeed, in contrast to all the other major Asian countries, one hears repeatedly of acute labour shortages, bottlenecks at certain times of the year and the consequent need to introduce various types of labour-saving equipment. The institutional arrangements in rural areas have succeeded in a short period of time in transforming China from a labour-abundant to a labour-scarce economy.

The central institution in rural areas, as described by Unger, is the production team, a group of 15 to 60 households organised into a production cooperative roughly coinciding with a village neigh-bourhood. The team is large enough to be able in most cases to exploit economies of scale in agricultural production and yet is small enough for the individual peasant to see a direct relationship between effort ex-pended and material well-being. Some activities, however, for example the provision of primary education and the management of small factories, cannot be organised efficiently by the team and accordingly become the responsibility of the brigade (which roughly coincides with a village) or, if necessary, the commune or even the county. At the other extreme, in contrast, activities which are best organised on a small scale—the raising of pigs, chickens and ducks; cottage industry; the gathering of wood or grass for fuel; the cultivation of some fruit trees and vegetables—are left to the private household. Thus distinct production and service activities occur at each level in the institutional hierarchy and the requirements of scale seem to be an important determinant of what is done where.

Factor proportions and technology do change over time, however, with the result that activities which once were best performed at a low level in the institutional hierarchy ought in future to be performed at a higher level. Technology and institutions can easily become out of consonance and this institutional 'disequilibrium' can be a major source of inefficiency. Hence the need for institutional flexibility.

The recent history of China is replete with episodes of institutional change, not to say upheaval. The redistribution of land to former tenants and landless labourers in the late 1940s and early 1950s was followed in close succession by the formation of elementary (first-stage) cooperatives, advanced (second-stage) cooperatives and communes. The progression was not linear, nor was it without failures—false starts, dangerous leaps and ultra-left experiments occurred in abundance—but there is no doubt that the institutional arrangements in rural China have been remarkably flexible and it is at least arguable that this flexibility on balance has contributed to efficiency.

Finally, the communal arrangements in rural China provide security to the populace. The family or clan no longer must rely solely on its own resources and those of the moneylender when illness strikes, when old age arrives or when harvests are bad. No one goes hungry. Risks are spread. Preventive and curative measures are taken by the community in concert. Clearly, a system which provides security and reduces risk is preferable to one which does not. Moreover, in such a system risky innovations and investments are likely to be forthcoming more readily and the costs and dangers of institutional change are more likely to be tolerated. Thus in the long run such a system is likely to be more efficient as well as more humane.

The institutional context evidently affects incentives and the general level of output, but it does not determine directly the composition of output. Let us examine some of the factors that do.

Grains, notably rice and wheat, are China's most important agricultural products and hence production incentives in rural areas must necessarily focus on these crops. The objectives of government policy are to produce enough food to provide an adequate diet to the entire population and to distribute a portion of that food to the cities where it constitutes the wage goods of the urban industrial labour force. The tasks set for grain policy have been facilitated by other policies affecting birth rates and migration which have resulted in a slow rate of growth of both the total and the urban populations.

The production teams, after consultation at the brigade level, are expected (i) to plant much of their land in grains and (ii) to deliver a fixed quota (which remains unchanged for 3–5 years) to the state at (iii) a low price. Production in excess of the quota (iv) may be sold by the team to the state at substantially higher prices. If rural households do not consume all the grain allotted to them, an allocation which is subject to a ceiling, they (v) often in fact dispose of the surplus on the black market.

Provided the quota is not set too high (and comments from informed observers indicate that occasionally it is) or if too high, is not enforced (which apparently it is not), the grain production-cum-quota-cum-pricing system has several advantages. First, it virtually guarantees that the basic needs of the population for food will be met. Second, it enables the state to appropriate part of the rural grain surplus at a low price which it can then use to promote urban industry. Third, it provides a very strong price incentive on the margin to increase grain output, since various reports indicate that 'high-priced' grain is 20 to 42 per cent higher than 'low-priced' grain.

Prices for output not subject to quota, i.e. subsidiary crops, particularly vegetables and the products produced on the small private plots, enjoy relatively high prices, thereby encouraging diversification on land not reserved for staples. Input prices, on the other hand, have been set rather low. Indeed, it is frequently reported that the demand for agricultural machinery and fertiliser exceeds supply, and it is possible that some input prices have been set too low for allocative efficiency; it is also possible, however, that the input pricing and rationing system has been used consciously to favour the less prosperous units and hence its modification could have important implications for the degree of equality. The terms of trade between agricultural outputs and inputs are not unfavourable to agriculture and have been improving, and this should increase incentives to expand production. In contrast, the terms of trade between agricultural outputs and manufactured consumer goods favours the latter, and this should provide a disincentive to expand the consumption of industrial goods. In other words, the set of incentives in rural China favours production and investment at the expense of consumption, and given the objectives of the leadership this set of incentives almost certainly has promoted efficiency in the utilisation of resources.

II. INCENTIVES AND EQUALITY

The incentive and payments system in rural China has five main features: (i) income from property has virtually been eliminated; (ii) income payments to members of a production team are often based upon the amount of work contributed; (iii) there is a reciprocity between contributions and benefits in transactions between units in the institutional hierarchy; (iv) small-scale private economic activity is allowed; and (v) emphasis is placed on local self-reliance.

These features are not immutable, nor have they been applied as dogmas. Emphasis on one feature or another has shifted from time to time and at any one moment different payment systems may coexist in different regions or communes. Broadly speaking, however, these five features apply throughout China and it is worth while enquiring how they affect the distribution of income.

(i) Except under rather implausible assumptions, a payments system which has abolished income from property is likely to be more egalitarian than one which has not. Thus on *a priori* grounds one would expect China to have a more equal distribution of income than most other underdeveloped countries, and of course she has. The land reforms obviously were of central importance in achieving this. The interesting question, however, is to what extent has the distribution of income been altered by the progression from a distributivist land reform to the construction of communes. Unfortunately there is not yet enough data to provide a definitive answer, but a careful study of the evidence which exists suggests that the distributivist reforms of the early 1950s were more significant than the formation of advanced cooperatives in 1956 and communes in 1958 in creating an egalitarian society.[2] If this view is correct, the effect of the communes may be primarily to prevent a subsequent re-emergence of inequality rather than to create a high degree of equality. That is, their role is to consolidate improvements in the distribution of income that were achieved earlier.

(ii) The principle of distribution according to work, if rigorously applied, is compatible with a high degree of inequality. In China, however, this feature of the payments system has not led to pronounced inequalities. There are several reasons for this.

First, the size of wage differentials is relatively low by the standards of other countries. Second, the distribution of collective consumption, particularly of education, health and other services, is divorced from the distribution of work-points and as far as one can tell is highly egalitarian. Third, as Unger points out, material incentives are tempered by moral incentives: members of collective units do take the common good into account in making decisions. Lastly, it is possible that with a falling birth rate rural China has begun not only to have a lower dependency ratio than most other countries but also a smaller variance of the dependency ratio. If so, this would help to ensure that a relatively egalitarian distribution of work-points was associated with a relatively egalitarian distribution of private consumption per head.

(iii) The principle of reciprocity in transactions between the units of a collective does tend to perpetuate existing inequalities. Once again, however, this principle is modified from time to time, namely, when 'periods of more institutionalised programmes' give way to 'brief attempts at radical change'.[3] As Unger says, 'during the several radical campaigns of the past decade, teams and brigades have been asked to contribute their resources and efforts without recompense' and, provided they are not asked too often or for too much, it has indeed been possible to improve the distribution of income between units by using labour volunteered by lower-level units to undertake large projects for the general benefit of the larger locality.

(iv) It is uncertain what proportion of income in rural areas originates from private economic activity and whether this activity tends to improve or worsen the distribution of income. Jonathan Unger guesses that nationwide 'a bit less than a quarter of the Chinese peasantry's income derives from private sources', whereas Aziz Khan assumes the figure is nearer 15 per cent.[4] Unger comments only in passing on the net effect of private activities on income distribution; G. B. Ng appears to believe that they probably are unfavourable;[5] while Khan argues that 'the distribution of income from private plots was probably more equal than the distribution of income from collective work.'[6] If this last view is indeed correct, then it is likely that it makes sense on grounds of equity as well as efficiency for the authorities to tolerate private plots and perhaps other private economic activity within the commune system. The fact is, however, that the effect of private economic activity on the distribution of income is not well understood.

(v) Finally, there is the emphasis on local self-reliance. Taken at its face value it would seem that a policy of self-reliance would tend to exacerbate existing inequalities. Under such a policy, to use Unger's words, 'the richer districts are well positioned to become further enriched while the poorer districts and localities remain mired in poverty.'

This would be true, however, only if there were no policies designed to reduce inter-commune inequalities. Yet we know that there *are* such policies.[7] For example, the county government can and does take into account the needs of relatively poor communes in allocating equipment provided by the state, in determining the location of infrastructure projects and through the location of rural industry. Similarly, the recruitment policy of local rural factories is designed in part to provide more remunerative employment opportunities to people from the poorest communes. Further, the poorer units are favoured in the allocation of credit, notably by the Agricultural Bank of China.

Thus one must conclude that on balance the payments system in rural China has resulted in a remarkably equal distribution of income, both within and between communities, perhaps the most equal in the Third

World. Considering only distributed collective income and income from private plots, i.e. excluding collective consumption, Khan estimates on the basis of a series of assumptions that 'the share of the bottom quintile is probably no less than 10 per cent while that of the top quintile is about 36.3 per cent.'[8] Moreover, although many have claimed to have detected indications of increasing inter-community inequality, there is little empirical evidence to support this conjecture and no reason in practice why the payments system (including taxes and transfers) should produce such a result.

III. ACCUMULATION AND TECHNICAL CHANGE

The majority of underdeveloped countries, as well as the now developed ones, have obtained the resources for accumulating capital by squeezing agriculture. This has not been so in China since the early post-liberation years. On the whole, price and tax policies in China have been used not to squeeze the rural areas but to 'inflate' them. Similarly, incentives have tended to encourage investment in rural areas (including housing) rather than the consumption of industrial goods.

The tax burden in agriculture is low, the level has been nearly constant for about a quarter century, and, because productivity has increased considerably during the intervening period, the rate of taxation has fallen steadily. The regressive nature of the agricultural tax is designed to encourage investment without, hopefully, offsetting the effects of policies described in the previous section designed to promote greater equality.

The Chinese place great emphasis on the importance of mobilising local resources and making investment decisions locally. This policy of decentralisation and self-reliance probably results in both more investment and more productive investment[9] being undertaken in rural areas than would be the case under a more centralised system. In particular, the institutional arrangements in rural China have been ideally suited to organising investment during the slack season in labour-intensive projects at low opportunity cost. In most cases teams supply labour for investment projects to the brigade or the commune in proportion to the benefits they will receive when the project is completed. In this way the principles of local self-reliance and reciprocity become mutually reinforcing.

In China, as elsewhere, the surplus generated in agriculture has been used to finance industry and the public services. China differs from many countries, however, in that a large part of the surplus appears to have been retained in rural areas. Industrialisation has been separated from urbanisation: many of the new small factories in China have been organised and financed by rural brigades. Indeed, Unger argues most interestingly that in the process of industrialising the countryside the economic base of the brigade has been strengthened and this has led to a strengthening of its political power and authority at the expense both of the commune and the production team.

A turning-point in China may now have been reached in the sense that opportunities for mobilising unemployed labour to undertake investment may be on the verge of disappearing. The end of the era of 'surplus' labour will require a different pattern of capital formation, a shift from capital-widening to capital-deepening, and consequently a greater concern with developing and introducing technological improvements. Now that labour shortages have appeared, more emphasis is likely to be placed on mechanical innovation. This will probably increase the scale of production, reduce the attractiveness of cultivating small private plots, contribute further to a shift of economic power from the team to the brigade and commune, and thereby help to strengthen the material basis for socialist agriculture. In my opinion, however, top priority will remain on biological and chemical innovations, particularly on fertilisers. The availability in China of a national source of relatively cheap energy, viz. petroleum, is likely to influence the type of chemical and mechanical innovations introduced and these in turn will have repercussions on the institutional hierarchy in rural areas.

Capital accumulation and technical change in China have been sufficiently rapid and well-managed in the last two and a half decades to produce an annual rate of growth of GNP of about 6 per cent[10] and an agricultural growth rate clearly in excess of population increase. This is a remarkable achievement, particularly when one recalls that the growth has been combined with a simultaneous and dramatic redistribution of income and wealth. These results cannot be attributed to the sudden birth of a new socialist man, but the mixture of individual and collective incentives, material and moral inducements clearly has been highly successful.

NOTES AND REFERENCES

1. Jonathan Unger, 'The Organization of Collective Incentives in the Chinese Countryside: Lessons from Chen Village', *World Development* (May 1978).

2. A. R. Khan, 'The Distribution of Income in Rural China', in ILO, *Poverty and Landlessness in Rural Asia* (Geneva, 1977).
3. See Unger's essay, footnote 14.
4. Op. cit., p. 273.
5. G. N. Ng, 'Rural Inequalities and the Commune System in China', World Employment Programme Working Paper, ILO, Geneva (Oct. 1976) pp. 20–3.
6. Op. cit., p. 278.
7. See, for instance, G. B. Ng, op. cit.
8. Op. cit., p. 234.
9. For an exception to this generalisation see Jonathan Unger, op. cit.
10. N. R. Lardy, 'Economic Planning and Income Distribution in China', *Current Scene* (Nov. 1976) p. 1.

First publication of these essays

The essays collected in this volume were first published as follows:

Chapter 1: *World Development* (Mar. 1974)

Chapter 2: *Development and Change* (Jan. 1977)

Chapter 3: *Bulletin of the Oxford University Institute of Economics and Statistics* (May 1970)

Appendix to
Chapter 3: *Bulletin of the Oxford University Institute of Economics and Statistics* (May 1971)

Chapter 4: *World Development* (May 1976)

Chapter 5: unpublished

Chapter 6: *World Development* (Mar. 1978); co-authored with Azizur Rahman Khan

Appendix to
Chapter 6: unpublished

Chapter 7: *Development and Change* (Oct. 1977)

Chapter 8: unpublished

Chapter 9: *World Development* (May 1978)

Index